Ek parvaaz dikhai di hai
Teri aawaz sunai di hai
Phir wahin laut ke jana hoga
Yaar ne aisi rihai di hai

GULZAR

THELOVEDIET

THE LOVE DIET

THELOVEDIET

SHONALI SABHERWAL

RANDOM HOUSE INDIA

Published by Random House India in 2014

1

Copyright © Shonali Sabherwal 2014

Random House Publishers India Private Limited
Windsor IT Park, 7th Floor, Tower-B
A-1, Sector-125, Noida-201301 (UP)

Random House Group Limited
20 Vauxhall Bridge Road
London SW1V 2SA
United Kingdom

ISBN 978 81 8400 377 2

Typeset in Adobe Garamond by Saanvi Graphics, Noida

Printed and bound in India by Replika Press Private Limited

To Mona Schwartz who taught me to follow my dream
And bought me to love Macrobiotics

To the man who taught me to love,
and loved me unconditionally:
My father

To all the men I have loved and still love;
who have made me explore higher levels of myself
and get to 'self love'

And to you, reader—may you find the answers to what it is
to truly love

Contents

Introduction

'Love is the law of God. You live that you may learn
to love. You love that you may learn to live. No other
lesson is requwired of man.'

MIRDAD

THE LOVE DIET IS BEAUTIFULLY summed up in this quote by
Mirdad—a spiritual teacher and counsellor. Mirdad goes on to
say: 'And whom, or what, is one to love? Is one to choose a
certain leaf upon the Tree of Life and pour upon it all one's
heart? What of the branch that bears the leaf? What of the stem
that holds the branch? What of the bark that shields the stem?
What of the roots that feed the bark, the stem, the branches,
and the leaves? What of the soil embosoming the roots? What
of the sun, and sea, and air that fertilize the soil?'

You are the Tree of Life. Your roots are everywhere. Whatever
be the fruits upon that tree; whatever be its boughs and leaves;
whatever be its roots, they are your fruits; they are your leaves
and boughs; they are your roots. If you would have the tree bear
sweet and fragrant fruit, if you would have it ever strong and
green, see to the sap where with you feed the roots.[1]

---

[1] *(Edited excerpts from The Book of Mirdad by Mikhail Naimy)*

To me, Mirdad's thoughts echo the central thought process of my book. I extend his analogy of the Tree of Life (you) having strong roots, leaves, boughs, and fruit—coming from its sap (blood) which is clean and not festered. Unhealthy blood will not attract love for another or take you to a place of 'self-love', but will cause you to only repeat the dramas surrounding love.

What makes for clean blood is the foods you eat. It is the thoughts you harbour because of the foods you eat, the air you breathe, and the lifestyle you choose to follow.

How did this book happen?

Love has many forms, but the kind of love that makes you selfless is born out of self-love. Sounds corny, right? But that's just the way it is. Self-love is the result of years of self-work and human evolution. My life has not been very easy. Relationships require a lot of hard work and learning how to self-preserve from heartbreak and pain. Still love is so wonderful; it's something we all want in our lives—we don't stop seeking it though we get hurt time and again and go through countless break-ups. When we fall in love again, we give the relationship all we've got, and are willing to stake our faith all over again. Ask yourself, can you love on a plane called the 'universal plane', where there are no negativities towards anyone—only pure love? I am not referring to only romantic love but all kinds of relationships.

The Love Diet is about this frame of mind and satisfied space that I find myself in after many years of emotional struggle and healing through the right kinds of foods. My friend Kamal always told me 'be an island unto yourself'. This was in the nineties and today I am just that—an island, green and rich with its calm waters around me; inviting only those relationships and people that bring in happiness. By this I don't mean to imply that relationships are a bed of roses; they are not meant to be. But do your relationships hurt you to the point of no return or do you look at them as learnings which help you evolve into a better, stronger person? That is the question you have to ask yourself. This book is a story about that 'space' of 'universal love'. What makes you love every moment of your life and the people that come into it with intensity and a compassion that comes from the core of your being? What makes love unconditional with everyone you come into contact with?

Men and women, both married and single, are facing more issues today than they did in our parent's times. You see more divorces than before—6 out of 10 of my friends are divorced. Single men and women in their late 30s and early 40s—some wanting to get married and not finding the right partners and some not wanting to get married at all. Married couples joking and laughing about how much intimacy there was in their marriage in the beginning and how it goes out of the window later. Divorced men and women not wanting to marry again, and on the other hand, some divorced men having more successful second marriages. And then there was me in all of this trying to figure out where I stood—married once for 10 years to my childhood sweetheart, divorced, and then single because I could not find the right partner. What was going on?

I tend to sort any conundrums in my life by taking to the literature written on it, and there is a lot out there which sends you in different directions. Also, along the way, I started writing for a men's magazine on subjects like relationships, intimacy, and the resulting issues between men and women, and this lead me to a book that explores the dimensions of intimacy, love, and sex through food and lifestyle for men and women.

You're probably wondering what food and lifestyle have in common and how are they related? Food and lifestyle go hand in hand and are the most essential ingredients in whipping up love in your life. Sadly, we don't pay enough attention to food habits and lifestyle in our lives. The thing is we have become so obsessed with being thin that being healthy has taken a backseat. While a few of us do recognize this fact, that percentage is very small compared to the rest of us living in complete ignorance as to what works for us in the areas of love, intimacy, and sex.

In the book *When Food is Love*, Geneen Roth says, 'Eating is a metaphor for the way we live; it is also a metaphor for the way we love'. She also talks about self-love and how it should be foremost in any relationship. For a lot of men and women, focussing on the wrong foods, or emotional eating as it is termed today, takes them away from actually focussing on themselves and each other, thus evading issues of love, trust, and intimacy. Geneen Roth says sometimes men and women would much rather lose weight than be close to another human being, or focus on their bodies than being loved. It's safer as they know where the pain will come from. Diets never work, as they can make you eschew the important foods and that hinders love and intimacy.

My book is about self-love first. It is about how your food through good blood condition and a cleaner body help you find the love in your life and keep it alive.

My story with love

My first recollection of love is seeing my mum and dad kiss each other when my dad left on a flight (he was flying with Air India). I must have been 6-years-old. I always saw my parents interacting with each other in the most loving ways. I never saw them argue or fight. And now that I'm an adult, my mom tells me they did have fights—just never in front of the kids. They had the ability to laugh at themselves, and a sense of humour. My mother has always had a mind of her own, so she was always having these healthy arguments with my dad. My dad use to say to me, 'No need to go to Prithvi theatre to see a play (we lived next door to Prithvi in a suburb called Juhu), we have a live act going on in our house every evening.' The best gift I think parents can give their children is a loving home and an awesome 'fun-filled' childhood, and that's exactly what I got. Unfortunately, this kind of love was to last only till I got married in my early 20s. I married my husband after dating him for 8 years. What went wrong in our marriage that lasted 10 years? In retrospect, I have only have one word to describe it—karma. I ended my marriage with a lot of love (universal love). A full-blown relationship only in my mid 30's—as my mum always says I lost out on my youth and to have ever know what it is to be truly loved by a man. But this particular relationship gave it all to me and I finally knew what it was to have my soul reflected back to me in his eyes. At the time I was in the peak of health and my food habits were all cleaned up. This technically meant that I was shining from inside which reflected outside. This relationship lasted only for 18 months, and yet I loved like I never did before, even after a 10 year period of sheer misery with love.

However, I look back at these years as a great learning experience. I have grown a lot as a person, and I left with a lot of love towards everyone involved in the marriage, including my ex-in laws and husband, and most of all towards myself. While I was married, my eating patterns were erratic, I had a stressful life, and I coped with compulsive eating sometimes to replace the love that was missing in my life. I knew my ex-husband could get up and walk away from me but food would not.

Cut to being single again, and having no time to get into another relationship. I was trying to get back on my feet again. I would classify myself as someone who is pretty serious and committed when in a relationship; being frivolous was not my thing. After my divorce, I was hung up on the first guy I dated for about 6 years; I didn't recognize the pattern of being a 'love addict'. The definition of a love addict is someone who is dependent on, enmeshed with, and compulsively focused on taking care of another person. This is where I was, as I had attracted a 'love avoidant' into my life yet again after doing the same in my marriage. It's a cyclical relationship...or, should I say, sick-lical. I was the one who was sick, he just played out his patterns. Imagine me literally going on in my head, 'Why don't you love me, please love me.' Rejection is a high and abandonment a horrific fear. I was clearly not dealing with myself effectively. So after waiting 6 years, I walked away from this one.

When you haven't been with a man for a long time, your friends give you all sorts of 'useful' advice. The advice is generic—one formula fits all. 'You know what you need, just some hot sex'; another friend said, 'You should be chanting to have sex soon.' I imagined myself chanting 'Please bring me a man, please bring me a man' and shook myself. It's not the lack of intimacy that's hard to accept when you are single. It's the patronizing concern of friends and family that is humiliating. My uncle from India for instance would ask me—'Met any Byrons in the Bay?' (I was in Byron Bay, Australia then.) Friends who end their e-mails with 'Any luck??' and others who sneak in a 'So, met anyone nice?' in the middle of a phone conversation.

When a woman is single for a longer period of time than is considered appropriate, there is all kind of pressure from friends and family. Though they are only concerned about our happiness and well-being, it's time we give self-love a chance.

Two years before my divorce came through, my dad passed away. To understand his cancer better and help him, I started studying Macrobiotics. In our very first meeting, my health counsellor said to me, 'Oh Shonali! You are too yang (in

Macrobiotics terminology, too contracted or too masculine). We need to make you more yin (feminine and soft) so you can attract a man into your life.' I didn't understand this comment. I was too 'yang'? And how the hell was I going to attract a man with what I ate?

As I started studying Macrobiotics and understanding how foods work with changing energies within one's body, I realized the profoundness of her statement. After following the principles of the Macrobiotic diet for two years post my studies, I experienced my own energies changing and I did attract a new man into my life. This time it was a great relationship. So my first full-blown relationship in my mid-30s and I was yin, feminine, and oh so happy. I managed to change my blood condition via food and became more balanced. By becoming more yin, I could attract love into my life and also manifest my dream of starting a Macrobiotic practice in India.

Nothing fundamentally went wrong in my relationship in my mid-30s, except our visions of what we wanted in the future. I wanted marriage and kids and he didn't, so we parted ways. By this time, my business had taken over, so my eating habits got erratic. I didn't veer off from the principles of what I espoused, but yes I started eating a little unhealthy. I met a nice guy, we had an emotional affair, and this was one of the hardest relationships to get over, post my marriage. I consoled myself thinking I was getting better with the amount of years I spent getting over relationships: I took 8 years to give up a marriage that was already over in the second year; the first guy I dated post my marriage took me 6 years to get over; and my first full-blown relationship which I manifested after getting on the Macrobiotic path took me 1 year. My friend Dilshad used to laugh and say, 'Shunu, you're getting better at this.' And as it happened, I met a guy who described himself as a gypsy, a wanderer, and at that point of time so was I. So we met over many wines, but I knew this was not me and we parted as good friends. This time there was 'no getting over time' required.

You're probably wondering where I'm going with all this? Judy Dench's character in the movie *The Best Exotic Marigold Hotel* says something lovely that echoes my thought process here—'There is no past that we can bring back by longing for it, only the present that builds and creates itself as the past withdraws.' Andrew Solomon, a writer on politics, culture, and psychology based in the US, says, 'There are no subtractive models of love, only additive ones.'

This book starts with love between men and women, men and men, women and women. But also, how can one be in a state of complete love? 24×7 love? How can someone have little or no negativity towards everyone, and learn to love from a universal plane perspective?

The book will give you the tools by means of the right foods and lifestyle to manifest love in your life at every level. Not just man-woman kind of love, but also to get to a space of self and universal love. It will help you lead your life with kindness and a cleaner consciousness and therefore, be free from negativity of any sort.

Part 1

Men, Women, and Evolution

'Universal life is like a symphony, while individual life is but a sound in this great melody, and, alone has no value at all. Individual man, like all animals and plants, is interdependent, relative to life everywhere. We cannot exist without our environment, without earth, without the sun, without the universe.

We should see, then, that we are the infinite universe which expresses itself through a form called the body.'

GEORGE OHSAWA

YOU MAY THINK I'LL START getting into the Adam and Eve drama but I won't. Looking at love needs a bit of understanding of men, women, and how they piece attraction and love together, before we delve into other aspects.

The order of the universe

We Indians call the universal energy or life force, 'prana'; in Macrobiotics terminology we call it the 'infinite universe' or 'ki'. Traditionally, it was said that man represents heaven and woman represents the earth. That's where the phrase 'women are more grounded' came from. The 'infinity' as we look at it is nothing but a 'oneness', a sort of all-embracing universal oneness. The universe does not remain in one state; it is constantly changing—transmuting all the time. It reminds me of something S.N. Goenka, who re-introduced Vipassana meditation globally, keeps reiterating in all his discourses—we as human beings are being born and are dying every day. The cells in our body die and are born anew. We are just matter, consciousness taken form, but our end is to be 'one' with the universal consciousness—that's when the cycle of birth and death ends.

In Macrobiotics we consider this oneness to manifests itself into two forms of polarity in all universal phenomenon—'yin' and 'yang'. Yin and yang are two viewpoints looked at in relation to one another. Modern day Macrobiotics re-introduced this concept as a dynamic practical tool for understanding phenomenon and things around us. For example, if you look at daily life, you can experience these two polarities in different ways. When you look at position—yin is outward, while yang is inward; In shape—yang is contractive, the tendency of yin is to be expansive; in direction—yin is upward, while yang is downward; in temperatures—yin is cooler, while yang is hotter; in dimension—yin pertains to space, while yang is more earthy; in weight—yin is light, yang is heavy; in elements—fire is yang, while water is yin. Looking at nature—the vegetable kingdom is more yin, and the animal kingdom is yang; yin is seen in nature in branches, leaves, flowers, while yang is seen in roots and stems. We Macrobiotic counsellors analyse you and your body organs keeping yin; and yang in mind; so softer and expanded organs like your lungs for example are yin; compact organs like kidneys and liver are yang.

Though we aim for oneness with the universe, perfect 'sameness' does not exist, nor does perfect symmetry—everything and everyone is a unique manifestation of the universe. Macrobiotic teachings, principles, and dietary guide-lines recognize factors common in us all and yet there are some factors that make us unique. We live on this planet, therefore we must adapt to its environment with our diet and lifestyle. We all share a common evolutionary background, and the result of it is our similar body structure. However, when applying Macrobiotic guidelines to an individual's life, their age, sex, activity, constitution, and condition are what make them unique and are taken into account as well.

EXAMPLES OF YIN AND YANG

ATTRIBUTE	YIN CENTRIFUGAL FORCE	YANG CENTRIPETAL FORCE
Tendency	Expansion	Contraction
Function	Diffusion	Fusion
	Dispersion	Assimilation
	Separation	Gathering
	Decomposition	Organization
Movement	More inactive, slower	More active, faster
Vibration	Shorter wave & higher frequency	Longer wave & lower frequency
Direction	Ascent & vertical	Descent & horizontal
Position	More outward Perihperal	More inward Central
Weight	Lighter	Heavier
Temperature	Colder	Hotter

Attribute	Yin Centrifugal Force	Yang Centripetal Force
Light	Darker	Brighter
Humidity	Wetter	Drier
Density	Thinner	Thicker
Size	Larger	Smaller
Shape	Expansive Fragile	Contractive Harder
Form	Longer	Shorter
Texture	Softer	Harder
Atomic particle	Electron	Proton
Environment	Vibration, air, water	Earth
Climatic effects	Tropical climate	Colder climate
Biological	More vegetable quality	More animal quality
Sex	Female	Male
Organ structure	Hollow, expansive	Compact, condensed
Nerves	More peripheral Orthosympathetic	More central Parasympathetic
Attitude, emotion	More gentle, negative, defensive	More active, positive, aggressive
Work	More psychological & mental	More physical, & social
Consciousness	More universal	More specific

Attribute	Yin Centrifugal Force	Yang Centripetal Force
Mental function	Dealing more with future	Dealing more with past
Culture	More spiritually oriented	More materially oriented

Source: *The Book of Macrobiotics* by Michio Kushi

Why opposites attract

You are the yin to my yang
The yang to my yin
From the depth of my soul,
I thank you for loving me
As I love you

EDWARD ESKO

Yin attracts yang and yang attracts yin. The attraction of opposites occurs everywhere and in all aspects of life. It's a dynamic live force that is present in life. For eg., atoms are formed by protons and electrons, or the magnetic field of a magnet. Another example is the hormones secreted by the endocrine glands which circulate freely throughout the bloodstream but only affect certain organs. These effects are due to the attraction force of a particular hormone matching the receptors on the cells of its 'target' organ in the same way a key fits a lock. If a hormone does not match a particular receptor, it continues circulating until it finds its receptor that compliments it perfectly. Adrenalin (yang hormone) binds only with the yin receptors that specifically match it.[1]

---

[1] Yin Yang Primer by Ed Esko

Sex offers a dynamic expression of this principle. Men and women have opposite energies; men receive a stronger charge of heaven's force and women a stronger charge of earth's force. Estrogen, the female hormone, is yin and it produces an expansive form in women and also a softer feminine form. By this I mean women have a softer, greater tendency to have expanded organs and an outward body i.e., a more expansive female form. On the other hand, testosterone, the male hormone (yang in nature), causes the male body to develop in a more cohesive and compacted way. The attraction between these two forces—heaven's force (yang) and earth's force (yin)—is the underlying invisible force for love and sexuality between men and women. Love is just another word for the attraction of opposites. So when we eventually get to men and women, the yin and yang is simple to see—men are yang (I can hear you say it) and women yin. I understood later what my counsellor meant when she said I was more yang and male-like—I needed to get to be yin and feminine-like before I attracted a partner in my life.

The Book of Genesis says, 'In the beginning, God created the heaven and earth.' This in itself shows that the oneness was split into two polarities—heaven and earth or yin and yang. Both these forces are complimentary and yet antagonistic. In the Upanishads, this principle finds meaning when expressed in the image of Brahma (universal oneness) split into Shiva (yang manifestation of this oneness) and Parvati (yin manifestation of this energy) or Krishna and Radha.

Just as opposites attract, likes repel each other. Yin repels yin and yang repels yang. When you boil an egg, heat, which is yang, is readily attracted to the egg white, which is actually yin. Heat does not get to the yolk first, which is actually the yang element of the egg. The white of the egg cooks faster than the yolk. Now to overcome the natural resistance of the yolk (yang) to heat which is also yang, a third factor needs to be added—another yang factor. This could be time (also yang), along with the heat (yang) that creates a double yang influence that overcomes the yolk's resistance. The yolk then breaks down and allows the heat to penetrate it to cook. As long as two likes are equally matched, friction or resistance will occur. When one becomes stronger, resistance is overcome and is replaced by attraction. The yolk changes its nature to yin with the added heat, so yang changes or transmutes into yin.

Once the opposites bond, they start to change. They become like each other. For instance, when men and women get married, the husbands become more domesticated (yin) and the wives become more assertive and dominating (yang). So essentially they take on the characteristics of one another. Over time, the polarity that brought them together becomes less forceful. Sex also brings this out—men and women in a relationship or married cannot keep having sex endlessly. They need to take breaks in order to re-charge their energies. Separation allows a man to reconnect with his masculinity and a woman to reconnect with her femininity. After a separation, they get attracted to each other with much more intensity. Parents and children are attracted to each other because of the differences that exist between them and the love and affection unites them. Children grow up and become more like their parents, and the natural attraction between parents and children becomes less, and often changes to repulsion. But this changes in later years to want for each other again and a sort of attraction between them.

So in a nutshell, whatever it is we seek—health, food, companionship, success, adventure—is to strike a balance with our present condition. There are days I crave to do my yoga practice (yin) because I have a frenzied lifestyle (yang) as opposed to going to a gym (yang) which I find manic. This is to bring about a sense of calm (yin) to my hectic (yang) life. So we are always attracted to what we lack. A period of intense activity will make you want to relax and vice versa. So yin changes to yang and yang to yin.

Striking a balance

I know you are wondering why I am going on about yin and yang and this whole theory about opposites and likes. This is to create a solid foundation, so that the principles on which Macrobiotics operate are clear to you. The principles which I will guide you back to are grounded in Macrobiotic theory and achieving balance is the cornerstone of this philosophy. Macrobiotics is the art of balancing yin and yang in our daily life so that we can successfully adapt to our changing environment. For eg., if you live in a hot (yang) climate, plants and animals tend to have an expanded (yin) form. While in colder (yin) climates, plants and animals have a yang or contracted form. Our health depends on our ability to adapt to our environment. When we don't eat seasonal or local foods, we lose the ability to stay healthy. While an excess of tomatoes may work in India (tropical climate), they may not work in a temperate cold climate. It's as simple as making our diet adapt to spring and summer by cooking light and using less fire in our cooking and reversing this in winter when we need heavier cooking styles, more fire, and getting the warmth from our food. The practice of this approach is based on the tenet that food is energy. Theories of modern nutrition do not take this aspect into account. Macrobiotics goes beyond the circumference of your plate and does not look at diet from just a carbohydrate, protein, and fats standpoint. It says foods have a subtle underlying energy that can change your energy— transmute it from yin to yang and vice versa depending on what you need. By balancing yin and yang in our diets, we can achieve long lasting health that will positively impact us and our relationships. Eating in this way leads to a peaceful mind. Our mind and emotions are a direct result of what we eat. For eg., sugar will throw you off, you will lose the balance of your mind; caffeine will do the same, as will excessive animal foods, making us rigid and more angry. Our mind and emotions are precursors to any sort of happiness in our lives. My Macrobiotic guru Mona Schwartz says, 'We (her and I) are missionaries on the road to Utopia because we are bringing peace to people's lives and showing them what true happiness really is. But true happiness can only be achieved in stages.'

The spiral of creation and the wheels of love

Yin and yang appear in the form of spirals of moving energy. They give birth to energy and movement, causing spirals to appear. When observing the polarization of the universal energy into yin and yang—the two antagonistic and complimentary forces that make up all occurring phenomena in time and space—the motion appears in the pattern of a *spiral* when viewed from the front. This spiral pattern applies to the growth of plants, to the currents in the ocean and appearance of winds on the earth, the flow of water, our fingertips, and the structure of our DNA. These spirals start with a yang, what we term centripetal force, starting outward and spiral inward once it reaches its so-called final compressed state where it turns into a centrifugal force expanding from this centre back outward. Remember these two forces—centripetal and centrifugal.

In the beginning, the universe—the spiral of creation— arose moving inward like a spiral through '7 orbital stages' (see diagram: Spiral of life on page 18). Everything in the order of the universe then appears in this ratio 7:1. The levels of consciousness in human beings also appears in 7 stages. The

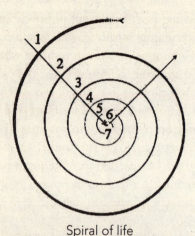

Spiral of life

Source: The Book of Macrobiotics by Michio Kushi

force of celestial influence that is showered upon earth day and night is 7 times stronger than the expanding force generated by the rotation of the earth. This 7:1 ratio appears in all natural phenomena; for eg., natural wave height and wave length maintain a ratio of 1:7 and the head to body ratio is 1:7. (See diagram Spirallic ratios in the human body on page 19). So if we were to relate this to the intake of daily food, drink, and air from our day-to-day environment then this is the ideal ratio to follow. For eg., the ratio of minerals to protein in the diet is 1:7; protein to carbohydrate is 1:7; carbohydrate to water is 1:7. Ratios are subject to change given the climate. Among foods, unrefined whole grain contains the ratio 1:7 of minerals to protein and protein to carbohydrate. A combination, for example, of an ideal diet and lifestyle representing this ratio of 1:7 wherein we take in the right food, drink, and air is soup, with some whole grain bread, cooked vegetables, beans, sea vegetables. some fruit, water, or herbal tea. **Seven-ness** is found everywhere; for example there are seven colours to the rainbow,

Spirallic Ratios in the Human Body

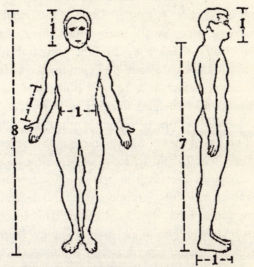

**The 7:1 proportion occurs in the
relation of head to body and other
ratios of the human body.**

Source: The Book of Macrobiotics by Michio Kushi

seven days to the week, and seven notes in the Western scale. It is believed that major life cycles run in periods of seven years each—childhood to age 7, adolescence at 14, adulthood at 21, 21 to 28 and so on.

The centripetal force comes from above and is referred to as the force of heaven and the centrifugal force comes from below and is referred to as the earth's force. In us humans, this heaven's force enters from above, that is the soft portion of the baby's head (again a spiral) moving downward. The earths force enters through the genital areas of the body moving upward. Both these forces create an channel of electromagnetic energy that we may call an energy channel or sometimes also referred to as the spiritual channel. In addition to these two entrance points, the forces collide and charge five major areas in the energy channel, producing altogether 7 major places of activated natural electromagnetic energy in the body. These energy centres are also called chakras. Chakra is a Sanskrit word and it was first documented in the Upanishads. (See picture on page 22)

The 7 major chakras are as follows: Muladhara (at the base of the spinal cord)—charging the testicles in men, and ovaries in women, as well as other reproductive organs and eliminatory system. This energy governs reproduction and regeneration. Svadishthana—located in the lower abdomen/sacral plexes—governs energy in the small and large intestines as well as bladder and genital areas governing digestion, decomposition, and absorption of food, water, and energy. This energy centre maintains body equilibrium and overall vitality. Manipura in the solar plexus region, governs energy to the spleen, pancreas and kidneys. Anahata at the heart centre, causes the formation of cardiac muscles, the rhythmical motion of the heart, and the smooth functioning of the entire circulatory system. It is in the heart chakra where heaven and earth energies are most perfectly balanced and if so, love happens. Vishuddha, located at the throat region, charges and activates the secretion of saliva, the vibration of the uvula at the back of the throat, as well as operation of the thyroid and parathyroid glands. Ajna is located in between the brow line, from where energy is distributed to millions of brain cells. Sahasrara is located at the crown of the head; this energy governs higher consciousness.

The 7 chakras or energy centres maintain and coordinate various physiological and mental activities in each region. Incoming streams of yin and yang forces branch out from the energy centres into 14 channels of electromagnetic energy called the meridians. The meridians, in turn, subdivide, supplying energy to all the organs, functions, tissues, and cells.

Our physical structure is nourished by a non-physical one. Energy comes from heaven and earth, and their charge gives life. In the chest cavity, the collision of these two forces causes our hearts to beat. Opposite hormones are secreted from the glands along the energy channel; some charged by heaven's force, others by earth's force. The meeting of these two forces also makes one breathe. So in reality our body is a spiritual entity. Cosmic spiritual force is constantly nourishing our consciousness, as well as our glands, organs, functions, tissues, and the trillions of cells that make up our physical constitution. These chakras are connected by pathways called 'nadis' or 'meridian lines' and if these are kept clean, then the chakras are charged positively. If the chakras are charged in this manner between two people wanting to engage in a relationship, then there is a stronger chance that a real connection is made. On our journey through our lives, the chakras are the wheels along this axis that take the vehicle of the self along our evolutionary quest, to reclaim our divine nature once again. The chakras are steps in the discovery of the self and take us back to self-love. In this journey, an encounter with our so called love partner propels us to complete ourselves and that's what the soul is eventually striving towards—completing its journey, merging with another to become one again.

On a physical level, the chakras correspond to nerve ganglia and to glands in the endocrine system (see diagram: Chakras and nerve ganglia on page 22). So they affect both the nervous and endocrine system. However, they are not part of the physical body, yet their effect on the physical body is evident. For example, an overblown third chakra would result in a big tight belly, while a constricted fifth chakra would result in tight shoulders. In metaphysical terminology, a chakra is described as a vortex, which is a mass of fluid with a whirling circular motion forming a cavity or vacuum in the centre which draws toward itself bodies subject to action. *Chakras* work with consciousness the way a vortex works with fluid. They spin in a wheel-like manner, attracting and repelling activity on their particular plane by patterns similar to a whirlpool. Anything that a chakra encounters on its vibrational level gets drawn into the chakra, processed, and passed out. The way we feel

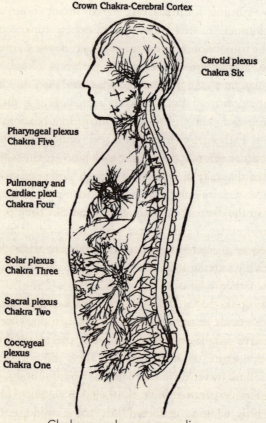

Chakras and nerve ganglia

Source: The Chakras, C.W. Leadbeater. A Quest Book, Theosophical Publishing House, 1972 ed.

influences the way we act. This impacts the kind of experiences we will have, which dictates the kind of energy we are likely to attract, which will in turn impact a given chakra. For eg., if we are low on self-esteem, this will impact our ability to feel good about ourselves, so we may attract a partner who will not treat us well. Our solar plexus chakra will record every action connected to feeling of low self-esteem and will spiral downward, not making it easy for us to get over this thought process. We need to recognize the pattern, stop taking mates who will treat us badly, and have more confidence in ourselves to strengthen the health of the solar plexus chakra. These chakras take into account not only actions from our day-to-day lives, but also the messages, and as I call it 'tribal rules', we get from our parents, in the conditioning, culture, physical body, situations we are born into, and information from previous lives.

I can almost hear you saying what this has got to do with love? Well, we need to move through each stage or each chakra successfully, learning our life's lessons to a place of self-love and then get to our fourth chakra, namely the heart chakra, which technically is where love emanates from. Unless this chakra is open, we seldom attract a partner who is right or meant for us.

The first chakra is called Muladhara (meaning root) and is located at the base of the spine, in the coccygeal plexus, and is about being **rooted,** giving us a foundation. Our feelings of security and safety come from this chakra. Any disorders with the large intestine and bowels affect this chakra—so this chakra needs to function well for our grounding in life. The second chakra is Svadhisthana (literally meaning sweetness), located in the lower abdomen, near the sacral plexus, and the purpose of this chakra is movement and connection. All our issues regarding **sexuality** stem from this chakra. It is related to our need to feel and experience pleasure. Any disorders of the spleen, pancreas, and stomach or menstrual difficulties in women will affect this chakra. The third chakra is called Manipura (literally translated as lustrous gem). It has the purpose of transformation, and is located in the solar plexus. Our need to act and be an individual and our feelings of *self-esteem* come from here. Any eating disorders, digestive disorders, diabetes or hypoglycaemia, chronic fatigue disorders of the stomach, pancreas, and liver affect this chakra. The fourth chakra is Anahata (meaning unstruck). It has the purpose of *love* and balance in our life. Self-love, our way of being intimate, giving and receiving in love also emanate out of here. Any disorders in the lungs, heart, breasts, asthma, circulation problems, and immune system deficiency affect the heart chakra. The fifth chakra is Vishuddha (purification). It has to do with our basic need to speak and be heard, to be a good listener; communication and creativity stem out of this chakra, as does our *will power*. Any disorders of the throat, ears, voice, and a level of toxicity in the body (as the chakra implies purification) affect this chakra. The sixth chakra is called Ajna (to command, or to perceive). It is located at the forehead in the middle of your brow, where the third eye sits. It has to do with establishing personal identity, and to see clearly. Our *intuitiveness,* capacity to be imaginative, and ability to visualize come from here. Headaches, vision problems, and obsessions cause this chakra to malfunction. Finally the last chakra is the seventh one called Sahasrara (thousand-fold). It located in the cerebral cortex region and its purpose is understanding, and the basic right to know and learn. Our thoughtfulness, intelligence, open-mindedness, and **being spiritually connected** stem from here. Any disorders of the brain, amnesia, and migraines affect the functioning of this chakra.

Now that you have been acquainted with the 7 chakras, you can cure yourself of most ailments by keeping them aligned and healthy. For each chakra to be functioning well, food, lifestyle, and the mind all play an important role and this is where I come in with this book. Besides, these variables, chakras respond to meditation, exercise, yoga, and then by changing mental patterns that we humans also get stuck in.

Falling in love

'Falling in love is nature coming in.
It starts with being carried off
By the opposite sex.'

JOSEPH CAMPBELL

The lower chakras create a physical desire to merge or have sex, while the upper chakras are active the very first time you meet a potential partner as your so called sixth sense, and level of intuition is at its highest. The two people so involved are already at a vibrational level with their chakras communicating more with each other. In terms of creating peace and feelings of congeniality between you and your mate, gentle and romantic speech causes the other person's chakras to relax and open up. When you conjure up a mental image of this person and you couple it with gentle speech, it activates the heart chakra. It is the heart chakra which is the centre of love, attraction, affection, and emotions. Chakra response normally begins in the upper body and gradually proceeds to the lower energy centres. When partners find each other attractive, these messages are relayed to the midbrain, where they create impulses and activate the meridians, organs, and endocrine glands, especially the pituitary. Activation of this gland stimulates secretion of the gonadotropic hormones, which in turn causes the reproductive organs to secrete the sex hormones. Visual attraction alternates between seeing a person's totality—actions and behaviour—and also looking at their character and physical appearance.

Sensing each other's energy is a subtle form of chakra energies getting exchanged. The quality of each person's energy emanating from the chakra determines if they will get attracted to one another.

Laws of attraction: just the 'two' of us striving to be 'one'

'Attraction and falling in love are love, but repulsion and separation are also love.'

MICHIO KUSHI

When we look at men and women, we see them also manifest these two polarities in their structure and outward manifestations of the body. For example, men have more hair and women less hair; men are left brained i.e., more analytical and rational, while women are more right brained i.e., they think much more, are emotional, and more intuitive. The term 'women are more grounded' comes from women being from the earth and aspiring towards heaven, and men beginning from heaven and wishing to be more grounded to achieve their dreams on earth.

Yin attracts yang and yang attracts yin—this is constantly at play between men and women. This creates the desire between them to want to be together mentally, physically, and spiritually. As the famous Macrobiotic guru Ed Esko says, 'Unity creates polarity, and all polarized things seek to reunite. Love is the cosmic process—a universal dance, a cosmic drama—that we see acted out again and again in countless forms among countless numbers of people.'

So essentially loves takes us back, albeit not completely but somewhat, to the energy of 'universal oneness'. Neale Donald Walsch, the author of *Conversations with God*, explains that relationships are our biggest learning ground. In a nutshell, we tend to attract people so different from us that essentially we look to our partners to complete us. According to various spiritual traditions across the world, the flowing circuit between two people in love is nothing but a path to enlightenment.

Most of us keep looking at our partners for a connection. We want to be loved, valued and finding this right connection can be an exercise in futility at times. Take me, I have told you my story in the introduction. I have partly dedicated this book to all the men I have loved in my life because they helped me to grow to newer levels of love for myself. It is through them that I learned to get out of so much negativity against myself to complete 'self-love' and appreciation of all the parts of my love. I fell also in love with 'me'. So essentially that's what relationships tend to do. Sometimes this happens just being with one partner who understands you and is on the same frequency as you. Yet today, more often you find people completely out of tune with each other. You'll find very few happily-ever-after couples, those who have figured out what makes them tick and why.

What's all this got to do with food and creating love?

Now that we have established how humans come into being, how energies of heaven's and earth's force come into play, manifesting in the 7 vortices of energy, and their impact on human sexuality and the laws of attraction—let's connect it all to how food is the answer. Doesn't it sound divine how food is the answer to all your love troubles? But not just any food—the right food.

The characteristics and functions of the human organism are exactly the opposite of plant organisms. Our lungs are compact and take in oxygen and give out carbon dioxide while a tree's leaves are expanded and take in carbon dioxide and give out oxygen. In human beings, the roots are located in our head. That's why in the ayurvedic tradition, the shirodhara treatment is used to nourish your roots—impacting your consciousness and higher states of being. This is where we also realize our dreams. The fruits and flowers (reproductive system) are at the bottom (see diagram: Opposite biological structure on page 29). The constant presence of ki vitalizes our cells. The real source of our life is coming from the universe around us.

The energy centres—namely the chakras—are vitalized by the blood that flows through your body which is charged electromagnetically. The blood depends on the quality and volume of food and drink that is consumed and the air you breathe. The energy channels can become blocked by eating wrong foods, overeating, or by foods which are nutritionally deficient. The environment around you also plays a huge role. For example, an environment that is chaotic, disorderly, or stressful will cause stagnation of energy. Foods also have an electromagnetic charge of their own in that the environment they grow in, the direction, climatic changes infuse 'ki' or 'life force' into food. Meditation also energizes your ki. When you meditate, you plug your charger to the power of the universe every day to vitalize your own ki energy.

The way I look at it, within the context of what your machinery is, it's important to know what makes for a cleaner body, therefore cleaner blood condition, cleaning up the network of nerve pathways within the body, so you attract the right partner. In the end, your own life force or ki has to be strong to invite the right partner and sustain your relationship on every level, be it emotional or physical.

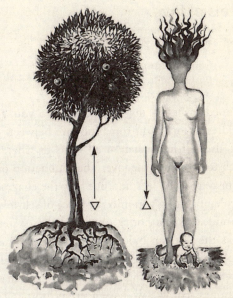

Opposite Biological Structure

A JUICY TIDBIT

According to research done by Syracuse University, twelve parts of the brain receive an intoxicating chemical cocktail when a person 'falls in love'. This download occurs within only one-fifth of a second after meeting someone; it's possible to experience 'love' at first sight.

The cocktail or chemicals released when a person 'falls in love' can lead him or her to make impulsive decisions. So it is wise for couples to stop themselves and check if things in a relationship are moving too fast. Actually listening to your parents, friends, and near ones can save you from a lot of heartache later on. If the relationship is meant to be it will go through this period and you will still be together.

The wheels of love

'To love one-self is the beginning of a life—long romance'

OSCAR WILDE

As I mentioned earlier in my introduction to you, this book not only addresses love as in romantic love between men and women but also self-love where it all starts or where we have to final reach to generate true love. The foundation of this lies in the chakra system. So let's find out how the chakras play an important role in getting you into the space of self-love.

Judith Anodea, an authority on the chakra system, refers to chakras as the 'human biocomputer'—as explained earlier chakra literally meaning 'disk'—and she extends the analogy of disks to the chakras to be thought of as floppy disks that contain vital programmes. For eg., we have a survival programme that tells us what we need to eat, drink, and the number of hours to sleep. It contains details such as how much money we need to make, what is a threat to our survival, and what makes us secure human beings. Likewise, we have programmes for sexuality, power, love, and communication.

Maybe I can extend this idea to a real story—a sad one—but true nonetheless. Before my dad got prostate cancer, he was terribly stressed for the two years preceding his disease. I mean really stressed. The stress stemmed from a property in which he had invested all his life savings post his retirement. The property was under litigation, and the matter was stuck in court for no fault of his. The builder had cheated people who had bought apartments in that building by double booking names on apartments. My father was a self-made man, and had earned all his money through sheer hard work. He retired comfortably, owning the property he was living in and set up a small business in his working years which kept his income rolling post his retirement. However, he invested all his savings in this one apartment and in his head it was now sunk. I used to keep telling him that he had plenty and my mum and he were happy leading more than affluent lives but to little effect.

My study of cancers and the manifestation of an issue in organs with reference to the chakra system explains this very well. When a man or woman suffers from issues regarding survival—money, sex, or power—these issues create stress which override the body's coping mechanism to deal with the amount of stress being generated. One will most likely manifest a cancer (as you start eating into your cell structure for the energy being used by the body and mind towards that stressful situation) in the second chakra—Svadhisthana—where the sexual organs are housed. A man will most likely take the hit in the prostate and a woman in her reproductive system. When I narrated this story in a quiet moment to my dad, he had tears in his eyes; but it was already too late for him—the cancer was in stage IV. My father had to learn to forgive his past, and the mistakes made, not hold grudges, and live with a compassionate love towards people (coming from the heart chakra) he thought were responsible. Instead, he did just the opposite. Above everything else, he had to accept himself for what he had done, and despite it all forgive his past and have immense love for himself. He couldn't bring himself to do this. His collective 'pain body' of his early years and having no money initially in his life was fully active and he kept identifying with it over and over again.

The chakra system is an evolutionary program and can be used to reprogramme our lives in the quest for healing patterns we keep repeating which manifest in ourselves and in creating the love we want. Like I had laid out, the Macrobiotic perspective on understanding life force and its split into two polarities—yin and yang, the chakra system also does just that.

When we talk of the chakra system, we talk of the 7 vortices of energy (the 7 chakras) created by the combination of two active principles—consciousness and matter. Just as heaven's force enters through the crown of the head, the flow of consciousness, as elucidated by the chakra system, enters through the crown chakra and moves downward through the body. This is referred to as *the current of manifestation*. For example, when we take thoughts and turn them into a visualizations, then words, and finally into form, we are engaged in the process of manifesting. The upward current which is the earth's force is referred to as the *current of liberation*. Human beings need a balance of both these forces in order to be whole and thus have stronger life force or ki.

Both currents are affected by negative experiences, childhood traumas, physical and mental pain, social programming, environments—these cut us off from the basic ground we stand on, and from the *current of liberation* that is the earth's force. In this cutting off process, our sexuality gets affected, and our self-power is manipulated. Our ground is our form without which we lose our individuality.

What blocks a chakra?

Diet, conditioning, belief systems, childhood traumas, repeated habits, physical and emotional problems, or simply neglecting a chakra that is facing issues will block a chakra. (See chart: on Chakra characteristics on page 33) Obviously since the body and mind are interlinked, we see this enter into our relationships, work, creative expression, and all these create negative repeating patterns.

Name	Muladhara	Sva-dhisthana	Manipura	Anahata	Vishuddha	Ajna	Sahasrara
Meaning	Root	Sweetness	Lustrous gem	Unstruck	Purification	To perceive & command	Thousand-fold
Purpose	Foundation	Movement, connection	Transformation	Love, balance	Communication	Pattern recognition	Understanding
Issues	Roots	Movement	Energy, Activity	Love, balance	Creativity	Image, intuition	Transcendence
	Grounding	Sensation	Autonomy	Self joy, relationship	Communication, creativity	imagination	Immanence
	Nourishment	Emotions	Individualization	Intimacy, anima/animus	Listening, resonance	Visualization, insight	Belief systems

NAME	MULADHARA	SVA-DHISTHANA	MANIPURA	ANHATA	VISHUDDHA	AJNA	SAHASRARA
	Trust	Sexuality	Will	Devotion, reaching out and taking in	Finding one's own voice	Dreams, visions	Higher power
	Health	Desire	Self esteem, proactivity				Divinity
	Home	Need	Power				Union
	Family	Pleasure					Vision
	Prosperity						
	Boundaries						
Location	Base of Spine, Coccygeal plexus	Lower abdomen, Sacral plexus	Solar plexus	Chest, heart, cardiac plexus	Throat, pharyngeal plexus	Forehead, brow, cartoid plexus, third eye	Cerebral cortex

NAME	MULADHARA	SVA-DHISTHANA	MANIPURA	ANHATA	VISHUDDHA	AJNA	SAHASRARA
Orientation	Self preservation Fear	Self-gratification Guilt	Self-definition Shame	Self-acceptance Grief	Self-expression Lies	Self-reflection	Self-knowledge
Demon Developmental Stage	2nd trimester to 12 months	6 months to 2 years	18 months to 4 years	4 to 7 years	7 to 12 years	Adolescence	Early adulthood and after
Developmental Tasks	Physical growth, Motor skills, Object Performance	Sensate exploration of the world, Locomotion	Realization of separateness, Establishment of autonomy	Forming peer & family relationships, developing persona	Creative expression, Communication skills, Symbolic thinking	Establishment of personal identity, Ability to perceive patterns	Assimilation of knowledge, Development of wisdom

NAME	MULADHARA	SVA-DHISTHANA	MANIPURA	ANHATA	VISHUDDHA	AJNA	SAHASRARA
Basic Rights	To be here & have	To feel, have pleasure	To act and be an individual	To love, and be loved	To speak and to be heard	To see	To know and to learn
Balanced Characteristics	Good health, Vitality, Well grounded, Stability, Feeling of safety & security, Comfortable in body, Ability to relax, be still	Graceful movement, emotional intelligence, ability to experience pleasure, nurturance of self & others	Responsible, reliable, balanced, effective will, good self-esteem, balanced ego strength, warmth in personality	Compassionate, loving, empathetic, self-loving, altruistic, peaceful, balanced, good immune system	Resonant voice, good listener, good sense of timing and rhythm, Clear communication, Lives creatively	Intuitive, perceptive, imaginative, good memory, good dream recall, able to think symbolically, able to visualize	Ability to perceive, analyze, and assimilate information, Intelligent, thoughtful, aware, open-minded, able to

NAME	MULADHARA	SVA-DHISTHANA	MANIPURA	ANHATA	VISHUDDHA	AJNA	SAHASRARA
	Right livelihood, Sense of trust in the world	ability to change, healthy boundaries	confidence, spontaneity, playfullness, sense of humour, self-discipline, sense of one's personal power, able to meet challenge				question, spiritually connected, Wisdom and mastery, broad understanding

NAME	MULADHARA	SVA-DHISTHANA	MANIPURA	ANHATA	VISHUDDHA	AJNA	SAHASRARA
Traumas & Abuses	Birth trauma, abandonment, physical neglect, poor bonding with mother, feeding difficulties, major illness or surgery, physical abuse or	Sexual abuse, emotional abuse, volatile situations, neglect, coldness, rejection, denial of child's feeling states, lack of mirroring, enmesh-	Shaming, authorization, volatile situations, domination of will, physical abuse, dangerous environment, fear of punishment, enmeshment, age inap	Rejection, abandonment, loss shaming, constant criticism, abuses to any other chakras, especially lower chakras, unacknowledged grief, including parental l	Lies, mixed messages, verbal abuses, constant yelling, excessive criticism (blocks creativity), secrets, authoritarian parents, alcoholic, chemical dependent	What you see doesn't go with what you are told, Invalidation of intuition and psychic occurrences, Ugly or frightening environ-	Withheld information, Education that thwarts curiosity, forced religiosity, invalidation of one's belief systems, blind obedience,

NAME	MULADHARA	SVA-DHISTHANA	MANIPURA	ANHATA	VISHUDDHA	AJNA	SAHASRARA
	violent environment, inherited traumas of parents: war veterans, poverty, survival fears	ment, emotional manipulation, religious or moral severity (anti-pleasure), alcoholic families Inherited: parents not worked out own sexuality	propriate responsibilities Inherited shame from parent	grief, loveless, cold, environment, conditional love, sexual and physical abuse, betraya	family (don't talk, don't trust, don't feel)	ment (war zone violence)	misinformation, lies, spiritual abuse

NAME	MULADHARA	SVA-DHISTHANA	MANIPURA	ANHATA	VISHUDDHA	AJNA	SAHASRARA
Deficiency	Disconnection with the body, Underweight, fearful, anxious, restless, poor focus & dsicipline, financial difficulty, poor boundaries, chronic	Rigidity in body & attitudes, frigidity, fear of sex, poor social skills, denial of pleasure, excessive boundaries, fear of change, lack of	Low energy, weak will, easily manipulated, poor self discipline and follow-through, low self-esteem, cold emotionally and/or physically, poor	Antisocial, withdrawn, cold, judgementa, intolerant of self & others, criticial, loneliness, isolation, depression, fear of intimacy, fear of relationships, lack of empathy, narcissism	Fear of speaking, small weak voice, difficulty putting feelings to words, introversion, shyness, tone deaf, poor rhythm	Insensitivity, poor vision, poor memory, difficulty seeing future, lack of imagination, difficulty visualizing, poor dream recall, denial (can't	Spiritual cynicism, learning difficulties, rigid belief systems, apathy, excess in lower chakras, materialism, greed, domination of others

NAME	MULADHARA	SVA-DHISTHANA	MANIPURA	ANHATA	VISHUDDHA	AJNA	SAHASRARA
	disporgan-ization	desire, passion or excite-ment	digestion, collapsed middle, attraction to stimulants, victim mentality, blaming of others passive, unreliable			see what is going on)	
Excess	Obesity, overeating, hoarding, material fixation, sluggish,	Sexual acting out, sexual addiction, pleasure	Overly ag-gressive, dominat-ing, con-trolling, need to	Codepend-ency, poor boundaries, demanding, clinging, jealousy,	Too much talking, talking as a defense, inability to listen, poor	Hallucina-tions,. Delusions, Obses-sions, Difficulty	Overintel-lectualiza-tion, Spiritual addiction, Confusion

NAME	MULADHARA	SVA-DHISTHANA	MANIPURA	ANHATA	VISHUDDHA	AJNA	SAHASRARA
	lazy, tired, fear of change, addiction to security, right boundaries	addiction, hysteria, bipolar, mood swings, crisis junkies, over-sensitive, poor boundaries, emotional dependency, obsessive attachment	be right, have last word, manipulative, power-hungry, deceitful, attraction to sedatives, temper tantrums, violent outbursts, stubborness, type A personali-	overly sacrificing	auditory comprehension, gossiping, dominating voice, interruptions	concentrating, nightmares	Dissociation from body

NAME	MULADHARA	SVA-DHISTHANA	MANIPURA	ANHATA	VISHUDDHA	AJNA	SAHASRARA
			ties Competitive, arrogant, hyperactive				
Physical Malfunctions	Disorders of bowel, anus, large intestine, solid parts of the body: bone, joints, teeth, Issues with legs, feet,	Inherited: parents not organs, spleen, urinary system, menstrual difficulties, sexual dysfunct	Eating disorders, digestive disorders, ulcers, hypoglycemia, diabetes, muscle spasms, muscular disorders,	Disorders of the heart, lungs, thymus, breasts, arms, shortness of breath, sunken chest, circulation problems,	Disorders of the throat, ears, voice and neck, tightness of jaw, toxicity (due to chakra's name, which	Headaches, Vision problems	Coma, Migraines, brain tumours, Amnesia, Cognitive Delusions

NAME	MULADHARA	SVA-DHISTHANA	MANIPURA	ANHATA	VISHUDDHA	AJNA	SAHASRARA
	knees, base of spine, buttocks, eating disorders, frequent illness	ion: impotence, premature ejaculation, frigidity, nonorgasmic Lower back pain, loss of appetite for food & sex	ulcers, chronic fatigue, hyertension, disorders of pancreas, liver, gall bladder	asthma, immune system deficiency, tension between shoulder blades, pain in chest	means purification)		

Source: Eastern Body, Western Mind: Psychology of the Chakra System as a Path to the Self by Judith Anodea

Releasing blocks in a chakra would involve:

1. Examine the personal history related to the chakra's issue—i.e. address what childhood trauma could have possibly caused the problem at the developmental stage. Understanding and going through this will reveal vital information about what caused the block

2. Balance excess and deficiency—i.e., if you are holding on to negative patterns and you cannot let go. For eg., you feel you are always being cheated on in life, this puts you in a situation of a money deficit all the time. If you are avoiding issues connected to the chakra you focus on them

3. Understand the dynamics of each chakra—i.e., understand the nature and characteristics of each chakra. We need to understand what the objectives of each chakra are and how to act to get them to function in an optimal way

4. Use your diet to clean the energy pathways connected to the chakras

5. Use exercises and techniques, meditation, visualizations to help un-block a chakra

We must acknowledge the demons that affect each chakra (see chart healing practices on page 46). These demons oppose the smooth functioning of the chakras. They also come up to teach us something, the fact that they appear is a reminder that we need to pay attention to them as they bring with them a gift, that of deteriorating the health of that chakra. If are scared and acknowledge it, we can transcend that fear.

Let me give you an example. Delna came to me with dark circles under her eyes and huge amounts of stress. She came to me because she wanted to be healthy and have glowing skin,

	CHAKRA I: MULADHARA	CHAKRA II: SVADISHTHANA	CHAKRA III: MANIPURA	CHAKRA IV: ANAHATA	CHAKRA V: VISSUDHA	CHAKRA VI: AJNA	CHAKRA VII: SAHASRARA
Healing Practices	Reconnect with body, physical activity (dance, aerobics, weights, running)Lots of touch, massage, hatha yoga, grounding exercises, look at relationship with mother, reclaim right to be here	Movement therapy, emotional release or containment as appropriate, inner childwork, boundary work,12 step programs for addictions, assign healthy pleasures, develop sensate intelligence	Risk taking (deficiency), grounding & emotional contact, deep relaxation, stress control, vigorous exercise, martial arts, sit-ups, Psychotherapy	Breathing exercises, pranayama, work with arms reaching out taking in, journalling, self-discovery, Psychotherapy where you examine assumptions of relationships,	Loosen neck and shoulders, release voice, singing, chanting, toning, storytelling, journal writing, practical silence, non-goal oriented creativity,	Create visual art, visual stimulation, meditation, Psychotherapy wherein you work with: colouring, drawing, working	Reestablish physical, emotional connection, Reestablish spirit connection, learning & study, Spiritual discipline, meditation, Psychotherapy wherein

Chakra I: Muladhara	Chakra II: Svadishthana	Chakra III: Manipura	Chakra IV: Anahata	Chakra V: Vissudha	Chakra VI: Ajna	Chakra VII: Sahasrara
		where you: build ego, strength, release or contain anger, work on shame issues, strengthen the will, encourage autonomy	emotional release to grief, forgiveness, inner childwork, code-pendency work, self-acceptance, anima-animus integration (male &female side balance yin andyang)	Psycho-therapy wherein you: learn communication skills, complete communication, letter writing, inner child communication skills, voice dialogue	ng with memory, connecting image with feeling, dream-work, hyp-nosis, guided visu-alization, past life regression therapy	you: Examine belief systems, Develop inner awareness, Work with higher power

	CHAKRA I: MULADHARA	CHAKRA II: SVADISHTHANA	CHAKRA III: MANIPURA	CHAKRA IV: ANAHATA	CHAKRA V: VISSUDHA	CHAKRA VI: AJNA	CHAKRA VII: SAHASRARA
Affirmations	It is safe for me to be here, The earth supports me and meets my needs, I love my body & trust its wisdom, I am immersed in abundance, I'm here & I'm real	I derserve pleasure in my life, I absorb information from my feelings, I embrace & celebrate my sexuality, I move easily & effortlessly, Life is pleasurable	I honour the power within me, I accoomplish tasks easily & effortlessly, The fire within me burns through all the blocks & fears, I can do whatever I want to do	I am worthy of love, I am loving to myself and others, There is an infinite supply of love, I live in balance with others	I hear and speak the truth, I express myself with clear intent, Creativity flows in and through me, My voice is necessary	I see all things in clarity, I am open to the wisdom within, I can manifest my vision	Divinity resides within, I am open to new ideas, Information I need comes to me, The world is my teacher, I am guided by inner wisdom, I am guided by a higher power

Source: Eastern Body, Western Mind: Psychology of the Chakra System as a Path to the Self by Judith Anodea

but did not realize that her kidney energy was shot, she was completely in a state of adrenal fatigue, and I could tell there was something blocked in her second chakra that housed her reproductive organs (she never spoke about this). As time went on, we kept tweaking her diet. I noticed that she was a bit obsessive about her diet, what I would call a health junkie. This was not normal, actually was a hindrance to her health. She overanalysed her diet and her physical self. I told her this a few times. One thing that really stood in her favour was that she was super committed, and got it all together with her diet. After a couple of months, her skin issues were sorted but I had to make her also address her fear which she was opening up about. She admitted she was harbouring fears though she never got into the whys, and said she would address them.

She met me after 3 months and her dark circles were gone (a clear sign that the body's adrenals were functioning better, and her blood condition was stronger). I thought this was it; we were done. But she wanted to sign up for another 3 months. During our nth conversation, I tried to address what she was holding onto that was impacting her reproductive organs. I did this by cross-questioning her, as I knew she was blocked in the second chakra. Sure enough, after some prodding she revealed she was trying to have a third baby and was having trouble conceiving. More importantly she revealed that she felt her husband was unfaithful and was holding grudges and resentments. *Ah, now it all falls into place*, I thought to myself. Her fear cut her grounding off (earth's force) and she developed a block in her second chakra as well as the first. Once I went through this with her, and also gave her some visualization exercises apart from addressing her diet, we were back on track.

All my adult years, as I moved through relationships, I realized I kept getting hurt. Even after reading so much Ayn

Rand, a leading proponent on 'self-preservation', I did not learn how to set up my own boundaries. I use to keep telling my homeopath every time that there was a physical manifestation of my emotional issue that I didn't know my own boundaries. I am a classic 'giver' in a relationship, sometimes at the cost of neglecting myself. This was during my pre-Macrobiotic days. By my third serious relationship (my average number of years spent in relationships is 6, which is 18 years of my precious life), I realized I was emotionally exhausted and repeating patterns. Enough was enough, and I had to address this issue. I was suffering from chronic lower back pain, and had stomach issues.

I used the knowledge of the chakra system and the Macrobiotic dietary principles to sort myself out. I know I had some issues in childhood as at one point as a child I thought my father did not love me. I am the first born child, and when my brother came along, in my mind the attention was taken away from me. My brother and I are two years apart. I clearly remember, at the age of 5, using one incident to judge my father saying to myself 'If he does this for me, he loves me' and poor guy probably did what he felt was right, not realizing how my 5-year-old mind was judging him. This is what set up my basis of some hurt, and a lot of jealousy towards my brother. To tell you the truth, my father loved me the most out of all three of us (I have a sister as well). He made no bones about it till the day he died. But hard though it is to imagine now, what I had walked away with at 5, affected me till I was in my early 30s. The physical manifestations of this were constant lower back pain and on an emotional front—very little trust in relationships, no sense of security, and some anxiety. That's what lead to the 'love addict syndrome' that I mentioned in my introduction to you.

I also sorted my issue by addressing the first and the second chakras . I used exercises (yoga) to help release blockages in these chakras and also did a lot of visualization exercises. See the chart for Chakra issues and question what issue resonates with your patterns. You need to first follow the diet to address your issues, and then the suggested healing practices and affirmations.

The loving heart

> 'Sometimes digging in the dirt and growing makes
> you a better person.'
>
> DR SUN WOLF

We must move through the lower chakras successfully in order to reach the heart chakra. For the purposes of the scope of this book, I have decided to delve into this chakra more deeply.

I'd like to echo the thoughts of spiritual teacher and author Eckhart Tolle here who talks about relationships:

'Unless and until you access the consciousness frequency of presence, all relationships, and particularly intimate relationships, are deeply flawed and ultimately dysfunctional. They may seem perfect for a while, such as when you are 'in love', but invariably that apparent perfection gets disrupted as arguments, conflicts, dissatisfaction, and emotional or even physical violence occur with increasing frequency. It seems that most 'love relationships' become love/hate relationships before long. Love can then turn into savage attack, feelings of hostility, or complete withdrawal of affection at the flick of a switch. This is considered normal. The relationship then oscillates for a while, a few months or a few years, between the polarities of love and hate, and it gives you as much pleasure as it gives you pain. It is not uncommon for couples to become addicted to those cycles. 'Their drama' makes them feel alive. When a balance between the positive/negative polarities is lost and the negative, destructive cycles occur with increasing frequency and intensity, which tends to happen sooner or later, then it will not be long before the relationship finally collapses.'

The key mention here is of 'their drama' which makes couples feel alive—this is where the sorting out has to be done. Very often we are addicted to our own dramas, this prevents us from moving on positively in relationships. There was a period in my life when I didn't know what it was like to be happy. It was as if being distressed all the time was my default mode. So much so that I think my cell memory got use to it. Then I decided to sort myself out. The cellular memory is the knowledge the cells carry about your existence. Each cell is aware of this memory which the scientists refer to as 'info-energy'; holistic practitioners say that this memory is not just restricted to this life, but your past life, conditioning, and experiences as well. If you think of your chakras as disks, then think of your cellular memory as the database stored on these disks in your cells. It is like your biological computer that will also impact your relationships and all that is happening to you. If your issues are not sorted out, your cell memory wounds jump up and re-create patterns for you—just the way I was used to being a 'love addict' in relationships.

Cell memory will affect your health if stress keeps eating you out. Cellular memory contains a positive emotion charge (PEC) and a negative emotional charge (NEC). PEC is our soul's birth right, which is an energy field that is alive, whole, peaceful, and non-fearful. NEC on the other hand, comprises of traumas, abuses, negative belief systems, and mental patterns. Eckhart Tolle refers to this as our 'pain body'—when the NEC becomes greater than the PEC, we experience problems in our mind and body and our 'pain body' becomes active.

Eckhart says, you can create drama when you are alone or with another person. When you feel sorry for yourself, that's drama. When you feel guilty or anxious, that's drama. When you let the past or future obscure the present, you are creating time, psychological time—the stuff out of which drama is made. Whenever you are not honouring the present moment by allowing it to be, you are creating drama. So be mindful of the present moment to stop this creation of drama.

Accumulated pain, as Eckhart describes, wants to survive, and it only survives if you unconsciously identify with it. It will then rise, take over, 'become you', and live through you. It feeds on any energy (negative usually) that you give it, anything that will perpetuate your pain: from anger, greed, being self-destructive, jealous, hatred, grief, and emotional dramas. Once the pain body takes you over, you want more pain. You become a victim or perpetrator. However, if you are conscious of it, the pattern would dissolve. The pain body, which emanates from the dark side (shadow) of your ego, is actually afraid of the light of your consciousness. Its survival is fuelled by your identification with it, as well as the unconscious fear of facing the pain. The moment you see it, and are aware of it, the identification with it is broken. You have found your inner strength and you have accessed the power of 'now'.

Tips to stop identifying with your pain body:

1. Breathe deeply, and bring your attention to yourself and your body
2. Be aware that it is your pain body. Don't negate it or judge it; just stay with it
3. Be present and an observer to it
4. Be aware of the pain, and you observing it
5. This is being present in the 'now'—what Eckhart calls 'the power of now'

It usually isn't easy, but can be done. Today after studying Macrobiotics and following it, I understand what foods help in creating negative patterns as opposed to positive ones and release chakra blocks. I have managed to sort my heart chakra and create love again in my life, and helped many clients as well.

So let's get to the heart of the matter:

Ancient tantric diagrams depict the heart chakra as a lotus of twelve petals containing six-pointed star made of two interlacing triangles. This represents the downward movement of the spirit into matter (heaven's force) and the upward liberation of matter into spirit (earth's force) meeting in perfect balance in the heart. Here is the final integration of spirit and mind with the body and soul. The heart chakra is the centre of love, as spirit and matter are combined here. As we Indians say, Shiva and Shakti are united here, in their eternal dance of creation, their love radiates and permeates all existence. Vishnu and Lakshmi take this on and are the preservers. They manifest in the middle part of our lives, bringing us steadiness and continuity. The love we feel at the heart chakra transcends sexual love. Our love at the heart chakra comes out of an acceptance of a place among all things; love comes out of a deep-seated peace, love which is not out of need, and something that comes with complete understanding of the self in harmony.

It is the kind of the love I have for you, while I am writing this book. I'm alone, sitting in Goa—I have moved here for a month to finish the book. I wake up every morning, meditate for an hour, cook my own meals, then write, and I'm happy in my solitude and with myself. There is a complete acceptance of my being in harmony with the environment, and this process of writing. I give to you in thought and words with love. That's the space I am referring to. In Macrobiotic terminology the heart chakra is a yin chakra—characterized by giving rather than demanding, a calmness rather than anger, pure love rather than animosity.

The Sanskrit name of this chakra is Anhata i.e., 'sound that is made by two things striking', as well as the meaning of unstruck, unhurt, clean and fresh. If your work has been done in the third chakra, it's easier to be in harmony in the heart chakra. The element which governs it is *air*, the lightest of all elements. It represents freedom, lightness of being, softness, and an expansion of love consciousness. Air also represents the breath—the bridge between the mind and the body; the oxygen with which we vitalize our cells; the prana, life force, or 'ki' as I have been referring to it in the earlier chapters. The heart chakra requires the breath for a physical and mental transformation.

Basic issues of the heart chakra

'Yesterday I was clever, so I wanted to change the world. Today I am wise, so I am changing myself.'

RUMI

Self-acceptance

The basic right of the heart chakra is to love and be loved. Any damage to the heart chakra wounds us tremendously and hinders the creation of love in our lives. It's one of the strongest human emotions, yet it is fleeting, when in fact it should be simple. We fall in love, make mistakes, get hurt, and yet if we have to do it all over again, we just go ahead and do it with the same intensity and passion. If we don't have healthy childhood experiences of love, then creating it in our adult lives gets difficult. Love is exactly as strong as life itself, as Joseph Campbell says. To heal your heart is to reunite mind and body, self and other into an integrated whole. Without love, there can be no integration.

The heart is blocked if there is no 'self-love'. If we are not intimate with ourselves, how can we expect to be intimate with another person? If we have no balance within, how can we maintain balance with another? We must be able to be alone, enjoy our own company, and treat ourselves exactly the way we expect another to treat us. Our partner's peeves with us are also essentially his/her peeves about himself/herself.

Nikki came to me with a weight problem; that's all she had underlined in her evaluation booklet (something my client's fill up before we get into a consultation). She spoke about how dedicated she was to her diet, how she was a health junkie, and obsessed with healthy food. Yet, despite trying a lot of diets, nothing worked. She had a cyst in her ovaries but never mentioned it under her health concerns. She had a digestive issue, and eating disorders due to obsessive dieting which also went unstated. Nikki's story revealed that she was carrying some shame—the demon of the third chakra. After some more probing, she divulged that she had been sexually abused as a child and she had carried this shame into her adult years. No fault of hers but her childhood trauma still haunted her.

For any transformation to occur in your heart chakra, you have to transcend the demon of shame. We have to value ourselves first, to value another. We must also learn to speak the truth if we are to heal and move forward.

Nikki went on and on about her weight, but was ignoring what her true self was going through. She had to bring her attention to her real self—that was her key. To enter the heart chakra, one has to reach a place of self-acceptance, self-examination, and self-reflection, which gets you to a space of self-love.

I got her to address this issue first. Sometimes it is just knowing the right switch; once that happens there is an energy shift, and the weight of your problem gets lifted—as Nikki's did. Of course diet played a huge role, but so did simply acknowledging her problem, being aware of her pain body. I gave her some visualizations in meditation that also helped in her path to wellness holistically.

Trauma and abuse in childhood

Most common cases of trauma that plague the heart chakra stem from familial relations, especially in childhood. We suffer because of distorted views of the relationship—like I thought my father did not love me. When such a relationship, which is one of the primary relationships in one's life, is viewed in a skewed way, then other love relationships become difficult to engage in or sustain. Many women tell me that their men do not put as much energy as they do in relationships. Men on the other hand feel that women live in their own self-created worlds where the men get neglected because of the kids and other things, and the whole emphasis on 'us' comes as a side order and not the main dish.

You have to look back to your childhood and examine how the trauma or abuse that you underwent affects your relationship with your partner at the moment. I have a friend who I keep saying has no emotions; he has never betrayed any emotional fabric in his nature. His mother left him when he was 10-years-old and from what I hear he was never hugged, cuddled, or loved as a child. In my view he suffers on a physical level from the lack of an emotional touch; he has trouble forming an emotional alliance with women, and his ideas of love are distorted. Children who are sexually abused form such distorted views about love in their lives as well. Like Nikki, they live in shame, so self-love becomes difficult and later on so would loving someone else. Harville Hendrix, in his bestselling book *Getting the Love You Want*, calls internalized relationship with our mother and father an *imago*. The imago is a 'composite picture of the people who have influenced you most strongly at an early age'. The images we carry are etched in our subconscious minds, and we carry them all through our lives. These relationships set the programmes we will play out with our love partners. By travelling down memory lane and going through our primary relationship, we can start becoming whole again, and break out of the negative programming we are carrying.

Rejection hurts the heart chakra. Like I said before, I was a love addict and rejection was my ultimate high. It sounds corny but it's true—a love addict will always look for a partner who will reject him or her. That is what keeps them going, feeds their 'drama' and superficial love for the other person. Rejection will fuel your self-esteem, albeit negatively, and create depression with love relationships. Again, a person who is suffering from this has to address issues in the third chakra first which houses self-esteem. Like my perception of my father rejecting me is something I carried into the latter years of my life. I was left with a negative self-image of myself, and found partners who fed that negative self-image. However, if we have important lessons to learn while unravelling the mysteries of the heart, then we go through the process more smoothly as I did. Rejection could start in the childhood years. Without the love of parents, a child wonders who will take care of him? Sometimes if we get rejected over and over again, we also tend to reject others. In my case, rejection after rejection made me wake up and address the issue. I had to endure lots of heartbreak, but I eventually addressed my demons.

Addressing you anima/animus

Colvyn, another male client of mine, thinks a man should be strong, show no emotion, be independent, successful, and chilled out. To him displaying emotion it is a sign of weakness and is in dissonance with his self-image. He has neglected his yin side, namely his feminine side. His partner Colleen bears the brunt of this, as he expects her to be the nurturer, and bring in the emotional balance into their lives—he expects the anima to come from her.

Joseph Campbell, a famous writer on mythology and spiritualism, says, 'When seeking your partner, if your intuition is a virtuous one, you will find him or her. If not, you'll keep finding the wrong person.' I have always known when I am going to meet a potential partner—there is an energy around them which I can feel, if I am in tune with it. The energy around them can be as simple as a non-verbal cue like a sign or a look. Campbell says this projection comes out of you—experiences that you have had and you are looking for to complete potentialities of the energies within your own system—the archetypal energies of the anima and animus.

'When anima and animus meet, the animus draws his sword of power, and the anima ejects her poison of illusion and seduction. The outcome need not always be negative, Since the two are equally likely to fall in love (a special instance of love at first sight).'

CARL JUNG

Carl Jung, the founder of analytical psychology, talks about the anima and animus. We develop the balance between the anima—the archetypal energy of the inner feminine more present in women (yin energy) and animus—the archetypal energy of inner masculine more present in males (yang energy). Both genders have some amount of both archetypal energies. Judith Anodea, an authority on the human chakra system, says 'Like a shadow, the unconscious anima or animus gets projected onto others, often in idealized states, wreaking havoc on our intimate relationships. If a man rejected his own feminine nature, he may abhor the feminine in other men while expecting his female partner to completely carry his concept of feminine, criticizing any independent assertive behaviour she might display. Women who claim they want a nice guy and then reject him when he shows feelings of softness are projecting their animus. If they can allow their own masculine side to increase, they can allow their men to be gentler.' Isn't it true that most often what attracts us in relationships, also tends to repel us later on when we get to know the person better. Thus, understanding our own projection of the anima and animus is important. You know your anima or animus by your response to the opposite sex. Joseph Campbell goes on to say that when a woman realizes that the power is within her, then the man emerges as an individual, rather than just being an example of what she thinks she needs. On the male side, when a man looks at a woman and sees only somebody to go to bed with, he is seeing her as a fulfilment of some need of his own and not as a woman at all.

Giving space

A major issue running in all relationships is the soul's need for attachment and the spirit's need for freedom. This is also reflected in modern times with more and more couples asking for space. My mother always says to me, 'I don't understand this concept; we never had this whole space business in our times.' However, she forgets how much she went on, in my growing years, about how she gave up her career to be at home, since my dad was the one flying around and away from base 20 days a month. While it was a conscious decision she had taken, she still kept harping on about how she regretted it, and a little bit of this was also directed towards my father. So her need for space (her spirit sought freedom), and soul sought the attachment she got from a marriage and kids. It happens to most of us in relationships as well; if our partner pulls away from us (not consciously), we tend to get insecure and want to cling to him or her. However, when our partner clings to us, we feel restricted and restless. So if you are seeking a healthy relationship, please recognize these dynamics. While they are normal extensions of the way you might act—it is always healthy to give one another space.

Handling grief

'When the violin can forgive every wound caused by others, the heart starts singing.'

HAFIZ

The definition of grief is the normal, usually sorrowful, reaction to a major loss. It is different from depression, which is a mental state in which sadness, loss, or frustration interferes with a person's daily life over an extended period of time. Most people experience grief following a loss but are not depressed.

Grief is the demon of the heart chakra; it inflicts most people who have a heart disease. A study done in the Journal of Clinical Endocrinology and Metabolism (April 17th, 2013) detected that those in the higher end of cortisol levels (measured through scalp hair, to monitor long-term cortisol exposure i.e. hair growth over 3 months) were more susceptible to coronary and cardiovascular diseases and diabetes than those who tested lower for cortisol levels being generated by their bodies. Cortisol is the stress hormone.

When we are hurt in love, we forget how to trust, and are vulnerable to feel rejected. I had an emotional relationship in 2010—this guy took me down an emotionally turbulent path (this I bring up with all due respect to him, and a kindness of the heart; all has been forgiven and we are in a place of 'universal love' today). We did not have a physical relationship (thank God for that), but I exposed my vulnerability by opening up myself emotionally and getting too attached. Relationships come to you to unlock your own dramas. And in that unlocking you are bound to get into your own 'pain body' state (as explained in my subsequent paragraph). An emotional build-up of attachment was more from my side, a 'drama' I had to 'let go' of. This relationship entanglement brought out my collective attachment issues with men in my life—I realized I had to address them. At that time I was reading a book called *The Palace of Illusions* by Chitra Lekha Banerjee Divakaruni. The book is a rendition of the Mahabharata from the eyes of Draupadi. In one of the scenes, she depicts the scene where Draupadi is put on the floor as a bet when the Pandavas are losing in a game of dice to the Kauravas. Once they lose, to shame the Pandavas, the Kauravas start disrobing Draupadi. The author has depicted the scene so vividly that I felt similarly disrobed emotionally. Sounds a bit dramatic now, but I identified very strongly with what she (Draupadi) went through emotionally at that time. This particular relationship created a lot of grief and pain, that my heart took a long time to sort out—but it was my issue, and my 'dramas', not this person's. My self had been wounded, and I felt unsafe. I identified so strongly with the grief that I compared it to what Draupadi went through! I had to cultivate a lot of compassion to heal myself and get over this wound. But I realized I was only feeding my 'pain body' which had accumulated memories of years of emotional attachment to other people. I had to learn to be more compassionate with myself and forgive myself of past wounds that I was not letting go. But the amount of grief that you can take on is tantamount to the amount of joy you experience in love on a negative polarity—so you can only imagine the wounds on your spirit and your soul. Use 'forgiveness' as a weapon to transcend your grief. If you genuinely forgive the other person for doing you wrong, you transcend the grief that is caused by them.

Pay attention to the following symptoms. If they have been present for more than a year after a loss or an incident, you need to address them as it is not normal grieving that you're going through. Anxiety, bitterness, agitation, feeling worthless, insomnia, emotional numbness, lack of trust in people, breathlessness, and not being able to detach from a person or a situation.

If you are suffering from grief because a relationship has ended, it will be hard initially but as the old adage goes—time is a great healer. You will miss the intimacy, the comfort, commitment, or even pure friendship. Thoughts like a bad relationship is better than no relationship are completely wrong as I found out in my marriage. Even though I had a Masters degree from the US and was a qualified Market Research specialist, I still didn't have it in me to get up and get out there, get a job, and move on. It took me years, and I remember my friend Dilshad saying, 'Shunu, everybody works, whether its rain, shine, sickness, or sadness. Just get off your fat ass and get out there.' But women are getting more independent, being alone is no longer a big worry, and believe me when I say this—it is better to be on your own than being in a toxic relationship.

So here are some practical suggestions to help you get over a break-up:

- Take some time off by yourself, allowing yourself to heal
- FORGIVE this person with love (do the forgiveness exercise given in the next section)
- Look at your dietary habits, don't overdo sugar or stimulants (alcohol, coffee)
- Make contact with all your friends, especially those with whom you have the least possible chance of getting into a sexual alliance

- Friends and family, as I mentioned in my introduction, will try to fix you up sooner than you are ready. Please resist all attempts to hook up with someone too soon
- Stay away from people you know in common for a while
- View your life sometimes as if you're having an 'out-of-body experience'—like it's not your own life; this will build some distance between you and your situation
- Laugh, watch old movies, or read something funny

Powerful forgiveness meditation

Close your eyes and imagine yourself standing opposite the person who has caused you grief. Now visualize a white light that extends from you to him/her. In your mind say, 'I forgive you for the hurt you have caused me knowingly or unknowingly, consciously or unconsciously, and I know you forgive me too. I love and approve of you and I know you love and approve of me too.' Now visualize yourself walking over to this person and giving them a hug as the white light envelops you both.

For an additional powerful verbalization, you can also say the following words. These are lyrics from a very well known mystic singer, Snatam Kaur. Recite these when you visualize the person who has caused you harm in front of you in your mind.

> May the long time sun shine upon you, all love surround you, and the pure light within you guide your way on.

As we work through the issues of our power chakras, being present in the heart chakra becomes easier, as does giving love. We connect to another or others in an expansive manner, with love that is all-encompassing. Love takes the emotions from the second chakra and balances it with the understanding of the seventh chakra. The energetic component of giving love is then nurturing. Here again I bring in the guru Judith Anodea who disects three ways in which you can heal your heart chakra: (1) as strokes in the forms and words of caring actions; (2) as an unconditional acceptance of people or things as they are; (3) as an underlying vibrational chemistry (affinity the person has something in their energy field that we need). By expressing love, we grow, we transcend, and we surrender to grow into more understanding and mature beings. We stabilize ourselves emotionally and find our own equilibrium.

Love, sex, and the chakras

When two people make love, the charge of energy along the primary channel (also called the Shushumna which runs alongside the spine. This channel is basically like an energy shaft and runs parallel to the other two channels—the Pingala on the right and the Ida on the left), intensifying, activating, and vitalizing each chakra and the functions they affect. The spark that occurs during orgasm flows through the primary channel, charging each chakra with an energy that vibrates through your whole body. It is usually called the 'chakra response'—since sex involves activation of the body's energy system, with chakras being in focus.

So when heaven's force makes an entry through the seventh chakra—the Sahasrara—it supplies energy to the cerebral cortex, activating images, consciousness, and sensations that originate from there. It then charges the innermost parts of the brain and the midbrain. From the sixth chakra—Ajna—it distributes energy to other parts of the brain. Brain cells process vibrations and act as communicative instruments. When you find someone attractive, this process has already begun. When two people make love, the most common, natural position is of the man being on top—this is because the male body is charged with heaven's force, which comes down upon the earth. The female body conducts the earth's force, which comes up from the earth towards space. The male controls the speed and intensity of lovemaking as his upper chakras are activated, especially the midbrain energy pathways.

In women, her 'hara' or Svadhisthana chakra is active, i.e. energy in her uterus. For this reason, a man's sexual activity is influenced by his imagination and that's how he can often have sex without being emotionally involved with a woman. However, a woman usually needs tangible and emotional love. Unless she feels loved, she finds it hard to enter into a sexual relationship. The vibrations of speech originate in the fifth chakra—Vishudha—at the throat. Communication between partners, flirtatious words, and softer voices all come from here. Gentle communication will open up this chakra, while harsh communication will not activate energy here. Touching each other before intercourse sends energy to the midbrain and then through the meridians under the skin. Chakras are connected by these nerve pathways called merdians or nadis (Sankrit). So any energetic exchange between partners needs the meridians or nadis to be clean for this energetic exchange. This is the reason that any part of the body can act erogenous if stimulated. There are also secondary chakras located in the palms, which get activated when couples hold hands. The energy primarily emanates in the heart and filters down to the palms, creating a feeling of closeness and warmth between partners. Kissing carries strong electromagnetic impulses through saliva, lips, tongue, and other parts of the mouth which are conveyed to the midbrain. Erotic kissing sends impulses directly to the sexual organs.

The heart chakra governs all our feelings of love, compassion, and emotions. The desire to merge with your partner comes from the second chakra (the Svadhisthana or hara) where the sexual organs are located. But the desire to merge with your partner mentally and spiritually comes from the midbrain, usually the sixth Anjna and seventh chakra, the Sahasrara. Earth's force causes the feelings and energy generated in the second chakra (hara) to move upward, while heaven's force causes the sensations produced by vibrations in the brain downward. These two energies merge at the Anahata which is the heart chakra, producing love—complete activation of energies and the nerve endings that are connected to it. When you fall in love, the sensation that accompanies it is that of expansion—lightness around the heart. When we say that one has 'heartache' due to a separation from your loved one, it actually means exactly that as there is a sensation of pain in the heart chakra. An embrace between lovers intensifies this expansion of love between partners. The breath is in the chest and when we hug our partners, our heart chakras meet and there is an exchange of energies, in effect surrendering the vibrations in our heart chakras to that of our lovers or partners, and also opening up our own heart chakra to receive theirs. The third chakra—Manipura—located at the solar plexus under the rib cage, translates feelings and sensations generated in the upper chakras to the lower areas of the body. When partners engage in sex, this chakra stimulates the spleen to contract, making more blood available to the circulatory system, increasing the capacity to absorb more oxygen. It also stimulates the liver to release glycogen, which is converted to glucose in the bloodstream. On a physical level, sexual arousal in women follows the intensification of earth's force along the primary channel and in the chakras. As earth's force gathers in the pelvic region, the lips of the vagina expand and part, and the vaginal walls secrete a highly charged fluid. The vagina also enlarges, but in a way that is opposite to the penis. Earth's force rises upwards and the energy causes the vagina to expand, while the gathering of heaven's force (coming downward) in a man's lower body and chakras accelerates the flow of blood to the penis, causing it to become large and erect. Heaven's force also enlarges the testes, and stimulates the man to rhythmically begin moving his lower body back and forth. It is when the concentration of these two energies reaches its peak that an orgasm is experienced. Chakras at this point release uncontrollable waves of energy, producing the orgasm.

Men and Women Speak Up

'The way of the miracle worker is to see all human behaviour as one of two things; either love, or a call for love.'

MARIANNE WILLIAMSON

EVER WONDERED WHAT HAPPENS WHEN love takes over? When both desire and love get intertwined and the magic these two forces create? Human beings have killed when not been able to reunite with their loved one, have changed their religion in the name of love, and have become outcasts to be with their beloved. Have you wondered how a man can be in love with his wife, yet share his bed with another woman? How do emotions take over and we end up making a wrong decision when we select a partner? How do couples continue to stay in love even when they haven't touched each other in years? How do men think of other men or women think of other women? Is it the same way as women and men think of each other?

Love on any level makes you happy; when in love with someone, it makes us come alive, and improves our body chemistry. Every time I have been in love, there has been a lightness in my step, every movement of mine was a dance, and I felt high on love and intoxicated with thoughts of the one I have loved. Ever overheard conversations in the women's bathrooms in the West? Most often it centres around men they have met, or someone that is attracted to them or some relationship they have just gotten out off or are getting into. I often thought it would be fun to have these conversations recorded.

What happens sometimes with this big bang in some of our lives which takes our energy soaring to the last floor of a skyscraper making us dizzy at the top, and also makes some of us get off before we make it to the fifth floor, and start the climb down the steps in a big hurry? Why are perfectly adjusted men and women sitting single? Why are so many married couples cheating on each other and living double lives? Why are teens giving in to habits which are detrimental to their lives, rather than building their lives. What is it that causes such melodrama among our teens today?

We are all looking for love—that's the consensus drawn. Some men and women may not necessarily want to get married again for obvious reasons, ranging from not wanting kids to not wanting to be tied down in a marriage; some may not want to be in a committed space at all—but ask any of them if they want love in their life and the answer to that is *yes.*

Women, of course, are driven by their biological clock when they look for a mate. I think this lasts up to a certain age. As I have seen with most of my single friends, once they cross the age of 43 they give up the idea of kids; therefore marriage is of less importance but finding a mate to love still means a lot to them. Most women approaching 40 still want to get married, and have kids, but love is still paramount in their minds. It's the same with single men—they want love, but many don't want marriage. Ultimately everybody is looking for somebody to relate to and complete him or her. All my single male friends who pretend to not want commitment, still want an anchor in their life.

I decided to conduct a survey of my own, doing in-depth questioning of men and women and what they have to say about where they are viz-a–viz love and actually creating intimacy in their lives. I have a Market Research background of 12 years, so I decided to do some in-depths (as we refer to them in the MR business) with open-ended questions. To some of you my sample may appear biased due to perhaps questioning people that I knew, or also people that fit a certain mental make-up (forced sample). However, I wanted an all-round perspective from married, single, attached, unattached, and not wanting to be attached men and women. For the purpose of this book, I just needed to go live with people to validate my hypothesis of 'self-love' being paramount in the whole process of creating love.

Mechanics of in-depths

Target audience: My target audience is primarily from SEC (Socio Economic Classification) A and B; which means they are Graduates/Post Graduates and professionals with higher income levels. They are also opinion leaders in a sense and doing extremely well in their chosen careers.

Age: 30+ men and women

Categories of division: Here's how I set it up. I made 4 categories to get a representative opinion and chose 10 people per category.

Category I: Married Men
Category II: Married Women
Category III: Single Men
Category IV: Single Women

** Among the married men, three had been married before. The same applied to married women. Among the single men, three had been married before. The same applied to women. There were two single gay men I interviewed, and two single lesbian women.

Let's find out what all of you had to say.

Apart from the emotional dynamics of what's going on with us, what do men and women think about love, sex, and intimacy? How important has self-love been? Why do the singletons want to still remain single?

Single women

A consensus that I drew was that all single women are looking for a companion. However, the single women who were not married were in a bigger hurry than the ones who had been married before. I found that 'age' and reproductive (child-bearing) period determined whether the single woman was looking for a mate that would bring in some financial stability. Financial stability in men mattered most to women if they were still in their child-bearing years i.e., mostly women under 43 years of age. To the women who were working, independent, and somewhat clear that having kids was not a priority— financial security in men was not necessary. Dating got 'old' as they grew older; it required too much of an effort and time. If, with time, two people connected, then 'quality sex' (as one of them described it) was what they were looking for. Two of them said that dating was actually fun and given their lifestyles and age (both 40+), they wish they could date and meet new people. Two of the lesbian women interviewed said dating was important; it was a good way to get to know the other person before getting into a relationship. Sex was also important to these women. Sex could mean different things at different times, in that, sometimes it could be a pure physical need, and then at other times you may form a bond with an individual. Both these women also mentioned that 'emotional intimacy' was a big factor in all relationships that were serious in nature. Without it there was no intimacy, and the physical aspects of the relationship did not last long. All agreed that sex was important, even though they may not be in a long-term relationship, but not sex just for the sake of having sex. One of them even mentioned that comfort and companionship are not always restricted to being in 'love' with a person. Sex is a great extension of a relationship that you share with another person, even if it's friendship. Most of them agreed that men are reluctant to be attached today. By and large, men are still looking for someone who is physically attractive, rather than what lies behind the looks. Plus, men who come out of long-term marriages that have ended in a divorce want to play the field for a while, and then realize it gets tiresome as two women also mentioned. Sex is easy and available as most of them said. However post 35, it's what kind of men you actually make a 'contact' that mattered to these women. Neither of these women was worried about ending up alone, minus a companion in their lives. What plagued their minds more was the thought of not being financially secure in their old age. One of them mentioned that a lot of marriages today exist where partners are anyways 'emotionally alone' and 'aloneness' need not necessarily be bridged by a companion. Three women also mentioned that being alone was a factor that got to them sometimes. They mentioned that a lot of the times, they had to make an effort to keep in touch with their married friends. Women who don't have age on their side are always in a hurry, pointed out by one who said her single friends were in such a hurry that their apparent desperation turned off men. All of them were happy professionally and felt the reason for them and many other women being single was that the old paradigm had shifted where women were subjugated by men. Two of them mentioned that men never wanted to be 'just friends' once it was clear that they wouldn't be involved—they would much rather not know the woman, than be friends with her. They all echoed the thought that self-love was of utmost importance and (as they had grown older), this factor mattered more and more to them and it helped them know themselves better, so that they would end up making the right choice in a mate. They were all aware that no knight in shining armour was coming to rescue them, and that they are all architects of their own destiny. A fulfilling, happy relationship meant a man sharing the same goals and visions and in the end being a friend to them. The lesbian women also mentioned that a partner needed to accept them for who they were and also who they were not. One of them mentioned communication as being the hallmark of a successful relationship. They all had one thing in common, and that was the more they came to understand themselves better, the more love they had for themselves. However, having said that, they also agreed that it made them more picky and choosy about what they wanted. All of the five women who were single (never been married) mentioned 'yes' to the fact that they may have wanted Mr Perfect when they were younger, and therefore may have missed the bus in their 20s and early 30s on account of not marrying 'Mr Good Enough'. They all felt that being healthy, attractive, and having a good attitude were important ingredients in attracting a mate.

Summary

- Single women are looking for friends in their partners
- Age and a woman's child-bearing years played a big role on how 'desperate' they are to get a mate
- Men being financially secure do not matter to those who are financially secure themselves. However, they do expect their partners to be committed to their work
- Dating gets 'old' and 'tiresome' as they grow older and the whole dating game becomes too much of an effort
- Sex is important, but not sex just for the sake of having sex; 'quality sex' is something that was of more value

- Emotional intimacy is very important in relationships, much more than physical intimacy
- Being 'alone' when they are old is not something that bothered them too much
- Knowing themselves and self-love is important in making the right decision in a mate
- They were looking for Mr Perfect when younger (20s–early 30s) and may have missed the boat

Married women

Trust, companionship, fun element, common interests, a sense of humour, their partners being pillars when they felt weak, a feeling of happiness and security, wanting to do for the other without expectations, and understanding were the ingredients these women mentioned for a good marriage. According to them, the concept of 'being in love' is not enough in the long term. One of them mentioned being on her own 'high' and having her 'own shine'. Marriage and love are multidimensional and evolving—attraction, friendship, support, and companionship form the bottom line. Of course the ordinariness of life sets in, children change the dynamics, but in most cases, commitment deepens the love. Married women should have realistic expectations, said one of them, as one cannot have what one wants all the time. A hurried and rushed lifestyle and kids do hinder time spent between couples, but unlike the West, most Indian couples are not giving each other that 'quality time'. One of them even said that in 90 percent of marriages, the husband will naturally say 'Why would I leave work? To go back to a sleepy family?' A lot of husbands come home to their wives in nighties ready to retire to bed, why then would men not go astray? While sex is like a tide that ebbs and flows, it is to be expected. Women should stay fit and attractive, and not lose their sex appeal after they get married or have kids. Sex is hugely affected if a man comes home after being out or works late. One of them says that when the husband gets home, he has come from an environment of work, business, and looks to unwind while the woman has to put the kids to bed and is looking to go to bed herself. Expectations are different. He probably wants to unwind by getting into something with his wife, and she just wants to hit the bed or it could be vice versa. She says, 'With all my friends, sex is a problem.'

All claimed that self-love and self-respect were important to them. Also important was keeping themselves motivated. One of them mentioned that every woman (not only married) should ask herself, 'Do we want to be mediocre or do better for ourselves?'. She said, it's like having a green veggie juice and asking yourself how you feel. A bad diet can play havoc with the mind; energy levels are important. One of them said, 'My life is a balance of everything I give of myself to my marriage. I divide my energy up equally between family, friends, children, diet, exercise and going out, so I achieve a balance for myself of everyone and everything I like.' One of them said that a little spiritual perspective always helps. 'Had I loved myself more when I was younger, I would have been more confident and had solid boundaries'. One said that 'high self-esteem' is paramount.

Giving space to each other in a marriage is very important for a marriage to survive nowadays. Women multi-task, take on a lot more, they need their 'time out', and they understand that their partners do as well. Financial independence is very important even if you are married today. 'While intimacy is good, so is space—it's good to have a balance between the two. I try to achieve and maintain a state of love and trust, which is a state of the heart and not so much the mind. It is important to love and not judge your partner,' said Vismaya, one of the married women I'd interviewed.'

For those who were married before, they said that their earlier experience made them wiser and more in tune with their negativities that surfaced in their previous marriages. So in turn, they dealt with their current marriages better. A lot of what you go through in the initial years of marriage is a growth in self-love. A woman married to a man who was married before said that being married to a divorcee (with a child) was not an issue at all. On the contrary, her self-esteem and being secure within herself were factors that made her handle his past life better.

Summary

- Trust, companionship, sense of humour, and lowering expectations is important
- Partners here don't make time for each other like they do in the West
- The mundaness of a married life tends to take over
- Sex is an ebb and flow, but in a marriage other priorities may take over like kids, parents, but sex is important
- Looking good, paying attention to one's diet, and being attractive must all be high priority even when you are married or have kids
- Giving 'space' to each other must take a front seat
- Being secure within themselves and knowing what they are all about are important factors

Single men

Love is overrated, and people get caught up in romanticized notions of love. What's worse is that women have too many expectations from men. Women want a complete package which does not exist. Love is not illusionary; it exists. But both men and women need to be realistic. One of them mentioned (he does not want to get married), being single gives him a delusional feeling of being the master of his own destiny. Another who is single but seeing someone mentioned that love did not just mean 'man-woman' romantic love, but more 'compassionate love'. When you are younger, it's 'attraction' and not love. The thought of accommodating someone else's constancy in your life is a space that he may not want to be in. Also, men need not conform to a societal norm of marriage and kids—'having children is sometimes an ego trip', and they really need to question if a marriage is what they really want. Dating may get tiring, but it is important, or else how will one meet various people to make the right decision. One of them said he enjoyed dating, but the pressures of work don't allow the dating to be fun anymore. However, single men do make time for it. One of them said, when one is younger, there are two kinds of relationships—one is just sexual, the other is more where one looks for companionship. When one is single, sex is a physical requirement; it is fun. However, when a man gets involved, love comes from companionship and a bond. This guy felt he was one for companionship and a bond, which should end in marriage. Two of them were very clear that they did not want to settle down (marriage) and what that revealed was the fear of being tied down and their space and time dictated by someone else (again this may be delusional, as admitted). Both of them said they did not need 'emotional intimacy' round the clock. If they could find partners who would 'nudge' them to change rather than expect it or force it, perhaps they would change. One of them, who was involved with someone, mentioned that even though he was involved, his freedom meant a lot to him. But he realized that sometimes (given that he is in a relationship) this might not be possible. While men are not built to be monogamous, if the women they fall in love with make them happy, then the question is will they do anything to rock that relationship? Will they step outside their marriage? Probably not. Dating is tiring, because of the expectations that women have of men. Women are far more liberated today, so things have changed in the dating context today. Men past 35 are looking at making a connection, and not just have meaningless sex. Also, none of them were worried about being alone when they were old. They felt being content and happy were more important factors than worrying about being alone. They were all happy being single; they said it gave them the opportunity, freedom, and ability to mix with different groups of people. There is no pressure of what the society imposes on you when you are a couple. While they do miss the companionship, they are grateful that they have great friends, whether male or female. They also felt women got into relationships thinking that they could change the man, and this was unreasonable. 'Change with change' is what should keep relationships together, not resisting changes in a relationship.

Among the gay single men, they mentioned that the gay movement is physically oriented; sex is a big thing. One of them mentioned that he doesn't date as he finds it tiring but sex is something he'll go in for if the person seems right. Besides, the movement has opened up a lot now, with the net bringing the gay community closer, and an openness in society towards gay couples. While emotional intimacy is something that is missed, both of them mentioned that they worked hard, were challenged constantly by his work, and a lot of other stuff kept them stimulated mentally like art, knowledge, and the creation of wealth, and one could be 'emotionally intimate' with so many other things in life. They had great friends and families who helped on the personal front. In the end, having a good friend was paramount.

Summary

- Love is overrated, people get caught up in the notion of romanticized love
- Women are expecting too much from their mates, and high expectations make men turn away
- One must question if one is getting married for the right reasons and having kids for the same as well
- Women are more liberated, and sex is more easily available. However they too believed that making a 'connect' was important
- Being content and happy are more important factors, than worrying about being alone when old
- Being single opened them up to meeting a lot more people from different walks of life, with no pressure of the 'couple' syndrome
- Single men not wanting to be attached in a marriage said that their notion that being single gave them some amount of control on their time, space, and life could be delusional thinking, but nevertheless is a priority for them
- Space and freedom mattered to these men, even if they were involved with a partner

Married men

Love is one of the strongest emotions, and one of them said, 'There are two things in life that are free—the air you breathe, and the love of your parents.' Marriage makes you take each other for granted, but in a very positive way. It's like you know your mother will always be there whether you spoke to her everyday or not, and it's the same with your partner. Companionship, trust, and compatibility are important factors. Friendship to one of them was the most important factor. 'You have to able to laugh at each other.' Everything changes from being romantic to now having responsibility. From being footloose, fancy-free to being more accountable. Decision making changes for two and then when kids come that gets extended. You have to 'change with change'.

It's not marriage that changes sex—any relationship that you have been in a long period of time will go through the same ups and downs in sexual intimacy. It's just that in a marriage, other priorities take over. It's not got to do with love, but priorities. Four of them mentioned that the passion in their marriages was still the same after spending an average of 10 years with their partners. If there is love for your partner, the intensity is always there. One of them said that sex actually gets better, as it grows into companionship, and is no longer sex just for lust.

Some said self-love was very important, and is the basic foundation of everything. One gave another view—to him it was very difficult to define self-love. Self-love stuff was for your own ego. In a marriage two people make adjustments, there are compromises and in marriages, and if 80 percent of your partner is good, the 20 percent is very easy to overlook. There is no 100 percent perfect partner situation. One of them believed that single men over 38 definitely had some 'chinks in their armour'.

People today are less tolerant of each other's limitations. When you are in a long-term relationship, it's a given that there will be bad days. You have to have the ability to stand it out. While having no time because of work or kids is an issue, this was faced even by the single man, and is a part and parcel of life—'that's just life' as one said.

Keeping it simple, having values and sticking to them, not overanalysing things too much, and making life easier for everyone around you, having strength of character—were all important determinants of success in a marriage. Another said he never felt 'old' or 'married' or like he was approaching '50'; he felt great about his life ahead.

Summary

- Although marriage makes you take each other for granted, it's in a very positive way
- Friendship in a marriage is one of the cornerstones in keeping it together
- Sex just gets better with companionship, and the intensity of passion actually grows over time
- Strength of character is an important determinant for a marriage to work out, and an ability to laugh at each other
- Being tolerant is a virtue one must cultivate
- Keeping it simple, not over-analysing, and just being happy are all important elements in a marriage
- Never feeling 'old' or 'married' like society defines it are also important
- Lifestyle issues like being too busy with work, or social commitments with time, are bound to be there. But for men who were married, that's a part and parcel of being married

WHY ARE MARRIED PEOPLE HEALTHIER?

Research indicates that married people not only live longer, but also have healthier lives. When couples are older, they indicate a higher level of satisfaction in their marriages, and also in their lives. Marriage does bring in a certain kind of decorum in terms of lifestyle. For eg., as married men indicate that they now have to consider decisions for two rather than just themselves. So as one of them said, partying, clubbing takes a back seat. Diets get more balanced and men are more careful with their health as are women, more so if there are children involved. Marriage has a positive effect emotionally and mentally as well. Building on a great relationship will decrease stress and increase your sense of well-being.

Sexual Dysfunction in Men and Women

When Aarti, a 27-year-old Mumbai-based event planner, first started dating her now husband Sahil, the two had sex almost every night. But after the couple celebrated their first wedding anniversary, everything changed. Sahil started brushing off Aarti's advances, often wanting to just watch television. The two of them kept up with their commitment of spending time together, going out for movies and dinners, and always kissed before bedtime and snuggled at night. Yet they were barely having sex. Aarti tried everything—from buying sexy lingerie to offering to do anything for Sahil. But nothing seemed to work—and it started to take a toll on their relationship. When they got into fights, Sahil would say that he just didn't want sex as much as Aarti did. He loved her but sex was not a priority for him anymore.

This is a scenario that you usually hear men tell you about women. So what's going on here with the role reversal? It is estimated that 15 to 20 percent of men suffer from hypoactive sexual desire disorder, which is persistently or recurrently absent sexual fantasies and desire for sexual activity. Durex, the condom company, conducted a survey where they found 37 percent of men have experienced a low libido at some point in their lives. Now as a counsellor I know taking anti-depressants and excessive medication can kill sexual desire and libido in men. However, research is also beginning to link it with lower dopamine (a hormone) which plays an important role in sexual desire. To add to this are factors like low self-esteem, stress, and job issues. Carolyn Myss, a medical intuitive based in the US, links all this the with second chakra, which houses the sexual organs. Sex, money, and power are issues which stem from here. Masculinity is tied to how much money you make, so often when you are not making enough, the libido plummets.

In a study conducted on Lifestyle/Dietary Recommendations for Erectile Dysfunction (ED) and Female Sexual Dysfunction (FSD) by a Urologic Clinic in the US, it was found that healthy behaviours are associated with a reduced risk of ED which is the consistent inability to attain or maintain a penile erection of sufficient quality to permit satisfactory sexual intercourse in men.[1] It has been estimated that the worldwide prevalence of ED will be 322 million cases by the year 2025. Similarly, FSD includes persistent or recurrent disorders of sexual interest/desire, disorders of subjective and genital arousal, orgasmic disorders, vaginal dryness, pain, and difficulty with attempted incomplete intercourse. It affects 30–50 percent women globally. In men, the study concluded that overweight contributed to ED, men who were more physically active were likely to be at a 30 percent lower risk of ED. The study attributed variables like normal weight, increased physical activity, not smoking, moderate alcohol intake, and less television viewing to be associated with good erectile function. In the case of FSD, a study done by the Boston Area Community College in 2005 indicated the

---

[1] Dario Giugliano and Katherine Eposito. 'Lifestyle and Dietary Recommendations for Erectile Dysfunction and Female Sexual Dysfunction,' Urologic.theclinics.com, 2011.

likelihood of sexual activity increased with physical activity (odds ration 1:84, high vs low physical activity level).[2] It was concluded in this study that 30 minutes of physical activity 5 days a week was associated with higher levels of enjoyment and engagement in sexual activity. Smoking and alcohol were found to be contributors to ED and less towards FSD.

As with men who suffer from prostate enlargement as a consequence of not having sex, women who abstain from sex also run some risks. Particularly in postmenopausal women, vaginal atrophy can occur. This condition could lead to dyspareunia, or pain during intercourse, creating a cycle of avoiding sex altogether. In addition, women who fail to climax may find sex less and less appealing, and the less sex they have, the more difficult it can be to ever experience an orgasm.

A Report of the International Consensus Development Conference on Female Sexual Dysfunction: Definitions and Classifications explained that female sexual dysfunction is a multicausal and multidimensional problem combining biological, psychological, and interpersonal determinants.[3] It is age-related, progressive, and highly prevalent, affecting 20 percent to 50 percent of women. Based on epidemiological data from the National Health and Social Life Survey, a third of women lack sexual interest and nearly a fourth do not experience orgasm, as E.O. Lauman and Rosen Paik say when they write on sexual dysfunction in the United States in the Journal of American Medical Association. Approximately 20 percent of women report lubrication difficulty and find sex not

[2] Lutfey KE, Link CL, Rosen RC et al. 'Prevalence and Correlates of Sexual Activity and Function in Women,' Boston Area Community Health survey (BACH), 2002-2005.

[3] 'Report of the International Consensus Developmental Conference on Female Sexual Dysfunction,' The Journal of Urology (2000).

pleasurable. Female sexual dysfunction has a major impact on quality of life and interpersonal relationships. For many women, sex is emotionally distressing and physically uncomfortable.

Dietary habits

In the same study (conducted on Lifestyle/Dietary Recommendations for Erectile Dysfunction and Female Sexual Dysfunction (FSD) by a Urologic Clinic in the US) it was concluded that diets that are followed by heart patients should also help with ED in men. When the subjects stuck to a Mediterranean diet of fruits, vegetables, monounsaturated fats, legumes, nuts, and whole grains, they had a lower incidence of ED and the same applied to women in this study. These results were compared to those subjects that ate meats and heavy saturated fat diets with a moderate amount of vegetables and plant-based foods.

Men in the test group were assigned to an intervention group and were entered into an intensive weight loss programme, involving personalized dietary counselling and exercise advice and regular meetings with a nutritionist and personal trainer. The dietary advice was tailored to suit each man on the basis of food records over three non-consecutive days, which had to be done the week before meeting with the nutritionist. Men in the control group were given written, oral, and general information about healthy food choices, but no specific individual programmes. After a 2-year period, men in the test group had lost significantly more weight than those in the control group, increased their physical activity, experienced favourable changes, and had a significant improvement in their ED. They also concluded that weight loss increased the overall perception of sexual functioning and increased sexual satisfaction in women.

Despite increased awareness of the importance of diet and lifestyle, there are large gaps in food-based recommendations and actual dietary practice of people. The increase in calories mainly come from starches from refined carbohydrates and an increased consumption of sugar and sugar-sweetened beverages like diet soft drinks, juices, snacks off the shelves and commercially prepared meals. A substantial body of knowledge demonstrates the adoption of a healthy lifestyle, including consumption of healthy diets and increased physical activity, conveys a markedly lower risk of coronary disease, thereby impacting ED in men and FSD in women, promoting a healthier life and an increased sense of well-being, and reducing the burden of sexual dysfunction in men and women. A large body of research points out to the fact that 90 percent of reported sexual dysfunction is not due to an emotional block, but due to an actual medical disorder related to diet.

From a Macrobiotic perspective, impotence in men happens when a man cannot generate sufficient charge of energy in the second chakra which houses the sexual organs. Energy blockages occur from the excessive intake of animal foods (this includes dairy) that are high in saturated fat and cholesterol. If the man is weak, then it's a result of an overconsumption of sugars, ice cold beverages, chocolates, too much of raw foods, and medication or drugs. Saturated fat will block energy pathways (nadis or meridians) inhibiting energy flow, which will impact a man's ability to get an erection and sustain it. During sexual arousal, nerves stimulate the *corpus cavernosum penis*—a pair of spongy muscle that contain blood flow during an erection. When blood vessels get lodged with fat and cholesterol, not enough blood will enter the penis as it gets blocked here. Men who suffer from cardiovascular ailments, high blood pressure, and cholesterol will be likely target for this going on. Yin causes expansion, so yin foods like sugars, raw in excess, medications, and stimulants will cause veins to enlarge and become loose, again impacting the holding of blood flow. The prostate in both cases will be affected. These also are factors that lead to erectile dysfunction and impotence in men. Also, overconsumption of flour products or refined flours constrict and tighten the chakras and blood vessels and generate mucous and fat throughout the body. Diet and lifestyle need to be addressed as that's what makes for good and sound blood condition, helping with the plumbing of your body working in top condition.

In November 2011, a French edition of the magazine *Psychologies* carried an article on how our food affected our emotions. They mentioned the Stelior School which is known for its research work in autism, schizophrenia, hyperactivity, depression, and multiple sclerosis. The study outlined the following foods that caused aberrations in the mind and affected emotions: *Monosodium glutamate (MSG)* a flavour enhancer used in Chinese cooking mainly, *aspartame* (a sugar substitute), *lactose* (a type of sugar found in milk), *casein* (a protein found in milk), *colour preservatives* (specially of the E kind), and *sugar*. These were known to interfere with brain function and cause mood disorders, apart from severe long-term damage if consumed continuously.

Sexual dysfunctions and lifestyle ailments

Most sexual dysfunction has a medical explanation, and usually a physiological solution. According to current estimates, about 30 percent of adult men and 40 percent of adult women suffer from some degree of sexual dysfunction[4]. Consider this scenario. You agree to have sex with your partner, but know that you will not achieve an orgasm. You feel you can do it, have planned it for the night, but your body seems to have lost a link in the sexual satisfaction chain. While you engage in it,

---

[4] University of Chicago Chronicle

you keep thinking you will get wet, but it doesn't happen. You go ahead with intercourse anyway and it is painful.

Consider another scenario. You've had a hard day at work and are tired. You hit the bed and your partner is in the mood. While you love your partner and want to respond and also get into it, you can't wait for him to finish and find that your body is just not cooperating with the whole sex thing. Exhaustion takes over and you just tell your partner to stop. What the hell is going on?

Stress in the bedroom and adrenal fatigue

Stress will reduce sexual desire and function. We humans have a flight or fight response to stress wherein energy is taken away from the digestive system and sent to our muscles. This will take away nutrients from your foods, which are necessary for sexual function. Also, in today's scenario we suffer from long-term stress and you can only imagine the situation we are in all the time. Another connection with the stress response is the adrenal glands attached to your kidneys.

Roy Fernandez came to me complaining of diabetes, high blood pressure, weight issues, and no energy for anything, so sex was out of the picture. He said he was tired of visiting doctors and did not know what to do with himself. He barely got a good night's sleep and craved a lot of salt, subsequently retaining a lot of fluid. What he did not see were the events that built up to the stage before he got his diabetes. He was clearly in a state of adrenal fatigue—something I see 80 percent of my clients going through today. I recognized it from my diagnosis of his kidneys running low on energy, and the typical symptoms one exhibits under such a condition. He talked about everything else, but the fatigue and low energy. Once I drew his attention to my diagnosis, he understood his predicament. We worked on his diet and corrected his lifestyle. His energy levels came back, and now he is maintaining his blood sugar levels and says the spark back in his bedroom.

Adrenal fatigue is the 21st century stress syndrome. Most people go from doctor to doctor trying to figure out what's really wrong with them, and since the doctors have no name for it and nothing shows up symptomatically, they don't have a prognosis or diagnosis for their clients.

Adrenal fatigue, also termed as hypoadrenia or hypoadrenalism, has been around for a while, but Indians seem to be suffering with it in abundance at the moment. Because adrenal fatigue has no magic pills to cure it, except diet and lifestyle, no

LOCATION OF THE ADRENAL GLANDS

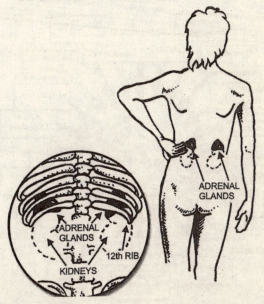

Source: Adrenal Fatigue: The 21st Century Stress Syndrome by James L. Wilson

one sees it as an illness that's afflicting people in their lives and also impacting relationships between men and women.

The purpose of the adrenal glands is to help your body cope with the onslaught of stresses (see picture on location of adrenal glands below). They are also called 'the glands of stress'. I remember my Macrobiotic teacher John Kozinski saying to us in class one day, 'If your adrenals are functioning well, you have the energy in the morning to "wake up and get going".' This is because the highest levels of cortisol are secreted at 8 in the morning, and this is why this cortisol is called 'rising cortisol' which helps us wake up in the morning. The adrenals give you the resilience to bounce back into life from a stressful period or

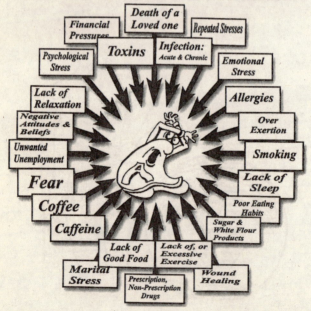

FACTORS AFFECTING THE ADRENALS

Source: Adrenal Fatigue: The 21st Century Stress Syndrome by James L. Wilson

situation, and also give you all your energy. They work on the hormones, sit on top of your kidneys, are the size of a walnut, and you can't imagine that they are your powerhouse of energy. They affect the way you feel, think, and perform every other function in your body. (see picture on factors affecting the adrenals below)

A deficiency in their proper function does not help release normal amounts of steroid hormones. They respond to stresses in your physical mental and emotional environment and too much stress in either of these start depleting them, and not only do the hormones secreted by them get affected, but what gets majorly affected is a hormone called cortisol. In a

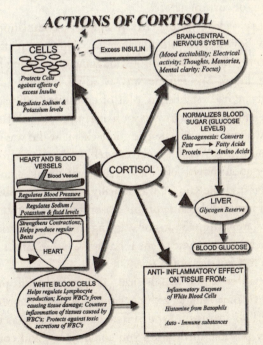

Source: Adrenal Fatigue: The 21st Century Stress Syndrome by James L. Wilson

serious case, getting out of bed may prove to be difficult. The more depleted your adrenals are, the more affected are your organs, and the more depleted is your sex drive, apart from the carbohydrate, protein, and fat metabolism in your body. People who suffer from adrenal fatigue have erratic sugar levels, like hypoglycaemia, and women will always exhibit premenstrual tension if suffering with adrenal fatigue. There will be a tendency to be fearful, anxiety-prone, confused, have bouts of amnesia, or poor memory. Once the condition gets worse, the body goes into a low-immune situation and then the tendency to get allergies, asthma, frequent colds, fibromyalgia, chronic fatigue, diabetes and other disorders, rises. (see picture of actions of cortisol before)

So here's another story. My friend kept complaining how her new boyfriend would not have sex with her. It had been four months and he was still just hugging and kissing her and nothing more. She felt he was avoiding physical intimacy, although he had established a lot of emotional intimacy with her. He had been out of town soon after they started dating for about two months and when he got back, all he did was give her a kiss and a hug. Weird, I said to myself, not getting into details with her about how I felt. I asked her if he drank, smoked, or did drugs and she said he was actually a teetotaller. She broke up with him, not because of this reason but due to some other stuff he bought up about not wanting to be in a relationship, etc. Much later he came to me for a consultation, and I got my answers to what was going on.

He had a series of physical ailments—blood pressure, anxiety, chronic fatigue, asthma, colitis had been depressed for long periods in his life, and suffered from insomnia. He was on every possible medication you could name, and could not live without it. His diagnosis told me he was completely 'burnt out' and in the highest state of 'adrenal fatigue'. He had this typical fat that men harness around their waistline, and the classic love handles. He preferred his own company to having sex as it involved too much energy mentally and physically. I also suspected he suffered from a bit of erectile dysfunction, which he did not want to discuss. We looked into his diet of course, but I had to also work on every possible front as far as his lifestyle was concerned. He had to be on some medication, but we took away stuff he was using as a crutch. He ate breakfast, lunch, snacks, and dinner from me. Along with that, I gave him home remedies for his nervous stomach and to normalize his sugar levels. We established walk times and some time for yoga. After a period of three months, he achieved some stability. He called me recently to say he is in a relationship and is happy (I assume in the bedroom as well).

The hormones that the adrenal glands secrete affect all processes that go on in your body. They also utilize carbohydrates and fats, and the conversion of fats and proteins into energy. They affect the distribution of fat around your waste (i.e., stored fat), blood sugar levels, and the functioning of your stomach. After you are in your mid-life, the adrenals also affect the sex hormones in both men and women. So they affect your weight and your sex drive. Many factors could affect stress.

So here is a bit of adrenal 101 and the hormones that affect your sex drive. Both male and female hormones are made in the adrenals of each person. In males, the adrenals provide a secondary source of testosterone and are the exclusive source of female estrogens (estradiol, estrone, and estriol). In females, the adrenals provide a secondary source of estrogen and progesterone, and supply testosterone. The linkage between PMS and a tough menopause and adrenal fatigue has been established by scientific research. Adrenal fatigue has also been positively linked to low libido. The vanguard to sex hormones DHEA, a pregnenolone, and androstenedione balance cortisol

HORMONES OF THE ADRENAL GLANDS AND THEIR ACTIONS

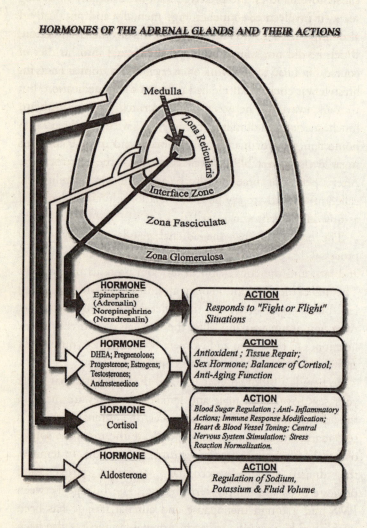

Source: Adrenal Fatigue: The 21st Century Stress Syndrome by James L. Wilson

as well and function as antioxidants for the sex hormones. Loss of libido is connected to the adrenals because of a drop in testosterone production in both men and women. You are less likely to be taken over by passion, when the body is in a flight or fight mechanism (survival mechanism kicks in). As we age, DHEA and testosterone levels start declining and so do the antioxidant effects of the vanguards of the sex hormones.

(See picture on hormones of the adrenal glands on page 96)

Quiz yourself to check if you have adrenal fatigue. Give yourself 2 points for each answer you say Yes to, 0 for each answer you answer No to, and 1 point for each answer you say Sometimes to.

1. I have a craving for salty foods
2. I find each task requires an enormous amount of effort
3. I find it difficult to wake up in the morning
4. I have a decreased sex drive
5. I do have feelings of fear
6. I tend to retain a lot of water in my body
7. I am constantly under stress of some sort
8. I am dealing with respiratory issues
9. I suffer from allergies
10. I tend to reach for alcohol when stressed
11. I have diabetes
12. I can't think straight under pressure
13. I tend to shake when I am nervous
14. I suffer from stomach issues (specially when nervous
15. My sleep does not relieve my tiredness
16. My muscles feel weak
17. I get headaches often
18. I suffer from low/high blood pressure

19. I have feelings of despair often
20. I get easily tired
21. I have low tolerance to people and things that don't get done
22. I am slow when I wake up in the morning
23. I usually sleep till late in the mornings
24. I suffer from skin problems
25. I have constant pain in my body
26. I have asthma
27. I have dark circles under my eyes
28. Women: I suffer from PMS (bloating, cramps, pain, mood swings)
29. I need coffee or tea to get me up in the morning
30. I crave meats, pulses, eggs, chicken
31. I do not exercise regularly
32. I have no sense of confidence in my life
33. I have joint pains
34. I am not a happy person
35. My nails are blue-ish or white in colour

If you have scored anything above 10 points in the Yes section you are suffering from adrenal fatigue, if you have scored 10 or more points in the Sometimes box then you are pre-disposed to adrenal fatigue. For those who have selected No as their answer for 5 more statements, you are doing fine.

Once you have discovered that you are a candidate for adrenal fatigue or suffering from it—what do you do? There is always a way out. The reason why I wanted you to establish if you actually did have some adrenal fatigue is to understand that with this syndrome, your life will suffer with your mate, partner, spouse, girlfriend, and all over. The good news is all of what you have to do to regain your health is in your hands. Your recovery will largely be dependent on your lifestyle, how you eat, how you conserve energy, and how you spend your energy. A large part of the recovery process is also how you clean your mind and thoughts.

Tips to manage stress better

1. Have a sense of humour—this gives you a distance from your situation

2. Communicate—to your partner or the person about feelings

3. Change your environment—like your job, gym, or toxic people

4. Exercise—release all those endorphins that will make you feel good

5. Consider going for counselling

6. Make a plan—draw three circles within each other, put the things and people that matter most to you in the innermost circle, and in the same way those that matter least to you in the outermost circle, and then those that are somewhere in-between in the middle circle. Get the picture right!

7. Visualize a pink bubble—now visualize the situation in its happiest form, or persons in their happiest form within that pink bubble, and release this bubble in the universe. See it fade as it lifts into the sky and goes up like a balloon and vanishes (in short, you are giving it up to the universe to handle it)

The adrenals and fear

Aparna is a social worker. She came to me as she said she had stomach issues (piles), dark circles around her eyes (kidney area), and no energy for anything. She had a live-in relationship with her partner, and they were happy; she had great friends, yet she worried incessantly about things and wanted everything to always be perfect. She stressed about the little things in life, being late to work when stuck in traffic, always anxious about disappointing people, and being angry. She always attracted trouble, she said, and had fear lurking in every corner.

As I analysed her situation, I realized that not only was she in a state of adrenal fatigue and her kidney energy was 'shot', she was also living in a consciousness of fear 24×7. She held this fear in her stomach, and her food habits were not great either. So she was manifesting stomach issues as well. Know this that the emotion of the kidney is 'fear' and this emotion deteriorates the kidneys, if one continues to feed it. Her cell memory was so used to it that she could not shake fear off. When you are in a state like this (the opposite of which is love), then you forget to love your near and dear ones, and generate love for yourself. Also, she had lost a sense of her own goodness and innate gentleness. A traumatic childhood or a painful experience can wire the brain differently to live out a pattern for the rest of your life. In Aparna's case, it was an experience she had with her mother being an alcoholic, and she lived in constant fear of her situation. Her mother had unpredictable behaviour patterns and would lose her temper at any time on her. She lived in this fear of her temper and mood swings 24×7, something her brain chemistry had gotten used to over the years.

You must bring in love the opposite of fear to your condition. Love towards yourself. Being aware of this 'pain body' of fear will release you from it. You may choose to go through it with a psychologist who helps you address this fear when it arises, and actually step into your mind, and question your thoughts. For eg. some help from friends, meditation, visualization, and sometimes re-affirming positive thoughts when a negative thought takes over also helps and deep breathing with a good diet in place should get you out of this. In Aparna's case, I did exactly all of this.

She said to me six months later that she would often get into situations of fear, but had started visualizing almost immediately and praying, that the higher souls would help her. I had taught her some heart chakra meditations, which she did, and she started loving herself more, something she never did in the past. Facing your fears is the only way to get better; running away from them is not the answer.

Stress, sex, and sleep

The '*honey, I have a headache*' syndrome is not the result of some excuse, but the actual truth of biology at play when you are stressed and fatigued on account of lack of sleep. Thick blood which is sludgy and not clean is the cause for headaches and also a sign that the body's pH balance is off. Research has indicated that quality of sleep is amplified to hitherto unknown levels by having sex. We all know how sleep deprived Indians are getting; it is said that 1 out of every 20 Indians is suffering from sleep disorders. Indian women (6.5 percent) outnumber Indian men (4.5 percent) by a 2 percent difference.[5] It is only during sleep that our body has the ability to repair itself, mainly from the amino acids (proteins) we eat during the day. Rapid Eye Movement (REM)—one of the five stages of sleep that

---

[5] Warwick Medical School on African and Asian Study of Sleep Problems.

lasts anywhere between 90 to 120 minutes and happens at least 4–5 times a night—strengthens our immune system and is considered a vital stage in the sleep cycle. So, technically, a good night's sleep will do the following for you:

1. Curb the body's inflammation: Inflammation is the body's mechanism to protect the immune system from trauma and usually results in joint pain, heart disease, and ageing

2. Increase the body's immune system response which will build organs and tissues

3. Affect you in a positive way psychologically by adding to your brains library of information, and helping you sort your life's experiences via dreams, gathering memories, and arousing creativity

4. Maintain healthy weight: Both sleep and your body's way to synthesize nutrients from food are controlled by the same areas of the brain

5. Builds the body's emotional reserves to combat depression better

The adrenal fatigue syndrome and its connection with thyroid

One of the key factors accompanying a thyroid condition is loss of energy and this in itself can cause problems in your sex life. The thyroid is responsible for producing several hormones, but two are absolutely essential—triiodothyronine (T3) and thyroxine (T4). These hormones take oxygen to your cells and are critical to your body's ability to produce energy. This important role in delivering oxygen and energy makes your thyroid the master gland of metabolism. Hypothyrodism— where the thyroid fails to produce sufficient levels of the thyroid hormones needed by your body—will slow down a variety of bodily functions, causing you to be exhausted and fatigued. Having mood swings, unnecessary weight gain and loss of hair (leading to a negative body image), and an abnormally low sex drive are symptoms of hypothyrodism. Hyperthyroidism occurs when the thyroid is overactive, producing more thyroid than is necessary. While hypothyroidism slows the body's metabolism, hyperthyroidism speeds it up. However, it still brings with it the symptoms of being tired, insomnia, hair becoming brittle, and loss of weight—all affecting your sex drive.

Out of all the clients I see, 60 percent have a thyroid issues. A lot of women come to me complaining about their weight and energy levels and 'hiding' behind their thyroid glands. You did this to yourself in the first place by taking on undue amounts of stress in your life, is what I say to them, now don't blame the thyroid for packing up on you, and don't hide behind it as an excuse either. I think one of the things I notice, as a health practitioner, is the lack of knowledge that people exhibit despite having access to Google at the press of a button. While I do not advocate too much of an information overdose, understanding how the thyroid functions is important to know how it will impact energy levels, affecting sexual energy.

It has been estimated that approximately 42 million people in India suffer from a thyroid disorder. While there are no statistics available in India linking thyroid to sex, a study that was released in the Journal of Clinical Endocrinology and Metabolism (USA 2010) revealed the following among hypothyroid men: 65 percent suffered from delayed ejaculation and erectile dysfunction; among hyperthyroid men: 50 percent suffered from premature ejaculation, 17.6 percent from a low sex drive, and 14.7 percent from erectile dysfunction.

An article published on the renowned health website WebMD said that 50 percent of women in the US suffered from some form of sexual dysfunction or the other and a large number of them also had a thyroid issue. Women with decreased thyroid function will eventually suffer from low libido. The good news in this study was that proper diagnosis and treatment got them to recover from tissues that are a result of thyroid disorders, impacting their sexual lives. Since these disorders can be treated with medication, your libido can bounce back with sound dietary and lifestyle changes.

Sex and blood sugar

Irregular blood sugar levels will affect your energy levels for sure. If we are getting in the simple sugars in our diet (processed flours, white sugars, refined foods), we will eventually suffer from the cravings, fatigue, and crashes that accompany it. Different foods convert into glucose which translates into energy for the body. As food is digested and the body metabolizes it, glucose levels in the blood rise, and trigger insulin—an aid that helps glucose to synthesize in our body. Different foods may convert fast or slow. For eg., refined white sugar converts very fast while a whole grain (brown rice or millets) takes a lot of time. If blood sugar is triggered by a fast acting sugar, then the rise and and fall is so rapid that there are peaks in our blood sugar levels and crashes; this is when energy peaks and drops. Complex carbohydrates are slow burning sugars, as are proteins. To add to this, processed foods with their hidden sugars are also the big culprits in modern-day lifestyle affecting our energy levels. Eating smaller and more frequent meals helps. Coffee, tea, alcohol, soda, colas all throw your blood sugar levels off. Diabetes has been linked to erectile dysfunction in men. So following the recommendations outlined in the later chapters will be good for you. Diabetes affects women by decreasing the blood flow to the vaginal walls. This may lead to the dry vagina syndrome and it may also change the pH of the vagina encouraging yeast infections. Women with diabetes do complain of feeling less aroused, having lower libido, and struggling to experience orgasms. It is not uncommon to go through mood swings, fatigue, weight gain, and a bit of anger if even your partner has these symptoms.

What's going wrong?

We live in a very ego-centric 'me first', fast paced, and overtly competitive world today. Sex has become a function and is no longer accompanied by 'chemistry' and a 'spark' that creates or makes for 'love' between people.

Here are some highlights from a survey conducted by Durex on sexual satisfaction:

- 84 percent of women have sex to get their men out of the house
- The average person has sex 84 times a year (that's once every 3-4 days)
- Almost 2/3rd of us don't feel we have sex often enough
- 48 percent of women fake an orgasm
- 44 percent are fully satisfied with their sex lives
- Those over 65 are still having sex more than once a week
- 82 percent reported that those who are sexually satisfied say that they feel respected by their partner. Mutual respect plays a vital role and is positively linked to sexual satisfaction
- 39 percent are looking for more love and romance
- 36 percent would like more quality time alone with their partner

- 36 percent would like better communication, more intimacy, and fun with their partner
- 29 percent would like a higher sex drive from their partners
- 37 percent want to feel less stressed and tired
- Only 29 percent of women orgasm while having sex
- 58 percent communicate what they actually want in bed to their partners
- 83 percent state they indulge in self pleasure at some point in their lives

> 'Sex is one of the nine reasons for incarnation. The other eight are unimportant.'
>
> GEORGE BURNS

Sex does form a basis of judging 'happiness' when it comes to couples. The more sex a person has, the happier a person feels. Men and women derive happiness from sex for sure, and those who have frequent sex have happier dispositions.

Look around you, Bollywood screams sex through their songs, so do advertisers selling juices (remember Katrina's lips in a juice ad), chocolates, love over the internet, hiding behind BlackBerry Messenger and WhatsApp, and conveying messages that you wouldn't have ordinarily done in person. Indians are no longer ashamed to talk about sex openly with their friends or in front of their family. Indians are having a lot more sex than they were before. However, how many of them are really having great, good quality sex—sex that builds intimacy in the long term—is the real question.

A joint research publication by Dr Blanchflower and Dr Oswald (when they were interviewed by the *New York Times*) on the economics of happiness, talked about a mathematical model by which they made the following calculations equating money and sex:[6]

- Great sex at least once a week is worth about $50,000 in happiness
- The emotional uplift of a long-lasting marriage is worth $100,000 in the bank, while a divorce causes $66,000 debit in happiness

Their study concluded that although greater wealth is associated with greater happiness, the wealthy are not having more sex. And, having sex with more than one person does not necessarily make one happier—a person needs only one sexual partner to be fulfilled usually.

I have gone through clients with issues on health and let me tell you from what I gauge in their diagnosis is that not too many of them have healthy sexual lives. We may be out of touch with our desire, but that does not mean it's not there. Traditional Chinese Medicine is of the school of thought that you can improve your relationship by improving the sex. To have better sex, to want more sex, you have to have sex. Having sex makes people and their relationships happier and better. Having sex quite literally makes love. Without sex two people living together are just roommates. The best sex is with someone you love and trust, and being in a strong relationship makes it even better. If you want more libido then you have to let it out more often.

The benefits of sex as we all know range from lowering your blood pressure, burning calories, releasing serotonin and oxytocin or the 'feel good hormone', also called the 'love'

---

6 David G. Blanchflower and Dr Andrew Oswald. 'Money, Sex and Happiness: an Empirical Study,' Scandinavian Journal of Economics, Vol 85 issue 4, November 2003.

hormone, keeping men's prostate healthy, making you live longer, look younger, busting stress, clearing you head up emotionally, boosting your immunity, aiding in great sleep, decreasing pain symptoms in the body, lowering the risk of cancer, and more importantly fostering a strong relationship (that's if you are seeking to do this with your partner).

There's sex and then there's 'good sex'. Good sex is about a great exchange of energies and a strong connection between two people. Both partners have to give and receive energy—it's a mutual flow of energies. No matter what tricks you get up to while having sex, without the exchange of energies between partners, it can never be satisfying. You can have great sex, and need not necessarily reach orgasm (the benefits of course increase with an orgasm); on the other hand, you can orgasm without good sex. It's all about creating a connection, when two become one psychologically, emotionally, and spiritually. If partners focus on rebuilding and rekindling this connection, they will have better sex and love lives. The answer to 'What makes for the best sex?' in a survey in *Playboy* magazine was 'Being deeply in love with your partner.'

The science behind falling in love: neurotransmitters

There are stages to falling in love, driven by a blend of chemicals called neurotransmitters which are basically brain chemicals that communicate information throughout the body.

> *Stage 1* Lust: Driven by estrogen, progesterone, testosterone, and acetylcholine
>
> *Stage 2* Attraction: Driven by adrenaline, dopamine, and seratonin
>
> *Stage 3* Attachment: Driven by oxytocin and vasopressin

Stage1: Estrogen, Progesterone, Testosterone, and Acetylcholine

A women's enjoyment of sex and her sexual libido is greatly affected by the healthy production of estrogen (and progesterone). Balanced estrogen levels provide for an overall feeling of health and vitality. Produced in the ovaries, the stimulation of estrogen comes from the luteinizing hormone (which is what your gynaecologist almost always tests you for if you go to get your sexual health check-up). Some estrogen is also produced by the liver, adrenal glands, and the breasts. That is why the health of these organs is so important. Fat cells are also responsible for estrogen which is why women are told to lose weight or put on weight before a pregnancy. Women with stuck 'ki' will suffer from either low estrogen or progesterone or vice versa. If you suffer from PMS, it's a sign of stuck 'ki' and estrogen dominance. Estrogen is absolutely necessary not just for vaginal lubrication but for happy sexual activity as well.

Low estrogen would make you go through the following:

- Pain during intercourse
- Vaginal dryness
- Low sexual libido
- Shorter menstrual cycles
- Heart palpitations
- Fatigue
- Sleeplessness
- Perimenopause
- Menopause
- Night sweats
- Hot flashes
- Poor memory

Healthy progesterone betters a woman's ability to relax both mind and muscles and for making healthy testosterone. High progesterone levels will make a woman go through the following:

- Mood swings
- Depression
- Weight
- Being irritable
- Headaches
- Breast tenderness
- Maybe acne and bad skin
- Bloating

Loss of libido in women is usually due to imbalances in estrogen and progesterone, sometimes endless dieting, and being on constant medication; smoking and alcohol consumption also affect this balance.

Testosterone also enhances a woman's sex drive besides giving men their muscles. Under stress, a woman's body converts progesterone to cortisol instead of testosterone which results in low sexual libido. Birth control pills inhibit the production of male hormones (androgens), including testosterone. Without testosterone in men, there is no sperm production and the blood circulation around the penile area is hindered. Low testosterone has been positively linked with erectile dysfunction. A man's testosterone declines with stress, medications, alcohol-abuse, drugs, and lack of sleep. Testosterone levels in men is absolutely fundamental to the health of his sperm, erectile function, and regulating desire. Signs and symptoms in men would include:

- Low sexual libido
- Chronic fatigue
- Erectile dysfunction
- Depression
- Poor memory
- A state of lethargy and general indifference

Stagnated 'ki' is also associated with elevated testosterone levels in women.

Acetylcholine is responsible for arousal; people with low levels of this brain chemical will suffer from lack of concentration during sex and lesser passion. It will herald the signal from the brain to your sexual organs while you are in a state of arousal.

Stage 2: Adrenaline, Dopamine, and Seratonin

Ever wondered why you go weak in the knees and your heart races when you meet someone you fancy. It's because the adrenaline (also known as epinephrine) in your blood and cortisol levels increase. It activates the sympathetic nervous system to increase heart rate and dilate your arteries to increase blood flow to your muscles during sex. Here, too, the adrenals come into play as during sex huge amounts of adrenaline are released into your system by the adrenals. That is precisely why your adrenals have to be up and running. Adrenaline makes you feel as if you are 'on a high'. It's a euphoric feeling, the kind you experience when you've had an orgasm.

A precursor to the release of dopamine is phenylethylamine—it is released during sex and peaks at orgasm. Researchers make a big deal of chocolate being the love drug because it has phenylethylamine. It makes you feel excited, happy, and hugely attracted to your mate. Dopamine, also known as the master molecule of addiction, is attached to the reward centres of the brain. It ignites this section of your brain with the intense onset of pleasure and is behind all addictions. In an experiment conducted on rats where they could push a lever to stimulate the portion of their brains on which it acts, they 'blissed' themselves till they dropped.[7] Excess dopamine has been found in people with cases of sexual fetishes. The craving neurochemical, namely dopamine, is the force behind sex, and foreplay creates the anticipation and sets the stage wherein there is an upsurge of this neurochemical. Dopamine is synthesized in the brain and adrenal cells, so yet again the functioning of your adrenals at optimum is very important.

The obsessive compulsive thinking about your partner all the time comes from serotonin, because every time you think about him or her, you feel good. Also serotonin is involved in the final phase of libido which is resolution. Seratonin helps modulate anger, sexuality, mood, and sleep. Low serotonin levels can put you in a state of lack of joy and decreased intimacy. While a bit of seratonin is good, too much of it will make you obsessive. This is why serotonin enhancing anti-depressants thwart romantic love and orgasms as they inhibit dopamine and norepinephrine and an elevated activity of both these neurochemicals are required to stimulate desire for your partner.

Stage 3: Oxytocin and Vasopressin

Ah, the wonders of Oxytocin! Oxytocin is known as the 'caring' hormone, also referred to as the 'cuddle' hormone, the 'love' hormone, or the 'open-hearted' hormone. This particular hormone drives your heart chakra. So I'd like to dig into it a bit

---

[7] Marnia Robinson in *Peace Between the Sheets*

deeper because the role of this hormone in love and bonding between the sexes is extraordinary. Without it we would never fall in love. It does the opposite of what stress does to you, and fights the elevated levels of cortisol that accompany stress. Oxytocin opens up our mind, allows us to focus, concentrate, and think. That's why they say making love is the best thing to combat stress. So cuddling, touching, caressing, and looking deeply into each other's eyes raises your oxytocin levels. Healthy oxytocin levels prove good for women as men can put off ejaculation if they have plenty of it.

On the other hand, elevated levels of endorphins are released when the body goes through pain, lowering oxytocin—like heartbreak will elevate endorphins and lower your need to bond (lower levels of oxytocin). Women who seek sex at this point must realize it's actually biology playing tricks with you as lowering of oxytocin reduces your need to bond, but you still want sex to recreate that feeling.

Another writer and neuroscientist Larry Young talks about monogamy, polygamy, and the effects of oxytocin in his book *The Chemistry Between Us: Love, Sex and the Science of Attraction.*[8] He studies the differences between a species of voles (animals resembling rats) with different sexual preferences: the montane voles are the serial daters, and engage in promiscuous relationships, while the prairie voles are monogamous in comparison. The prairie voles have additional receptors for oxytocin in an area of the brain called nucleus accumbens (NAC). Oxytocin sharpens their response to social stimuli, reinforced by dopamine in this area of the brain. The prairie voles have convergences of dopamine and reward learning as they get input from social cues from their partners, which fosters

---

[8] Larry Young. *The Chemistry Between Us: Love, Sex and the Science of Attraction.* Penguin USA, 2012.

association towards them. While oxytocin has some role in this bonding, so does vasopressin (released by the hypothalamus). This area, namely the NAC, is concerned with reward and reinforcement. Since this area decodes neural signs of the partner, like let's say body odour, it gets reinforced, and prairie voles react to these cues of their partners all the time. Both oxytocin and vasopressin are released by the pituitary gland; hence the proper functioning of your thyroid becomes crucial.

Vasopressin is also called the 'monogamy molecule'. It creates a desire in the male to stay with his mate (so women out there make sure your man has plenty of it). It also motivates him to protect his territory as he sees woman as an extension of himself. Vasopressin keeps your mate (males) monogamous. It keeps them loyal and makes them jealous when another man shows his affection for you. The prarie voles that Larry Young studied also have healthy doses of vasopressin. Several studies confirm that the 'commitment phobes' usually have a genetic variation in vasopressin receptors.

Vasopressin is known to increase sexual receptivity in women and aids in erection of the penis, so quite literally without it there would be no sundae, leave alone the cherry on it. It will foster monogamy, attraction, and keep you together even after the 4- or 7-year itch. Without it, you will feel unloved or even unloving. Oxytocin is why there is love in your life in the first place.

In a study done by the journal *Social, Cognitive and Affective Neuroscience* (SCAN) in 2012, men and women were given a dose of oxytocin before facing a disagreeable situation between themselves. The research involved 47 heterosexual couples that were either married or living together, who were happy in relationships, and not seeking therapy. Before being given oxytocin or the placebo, they were told to pick two areas that were disagreeable in their relationship. After the oxytocin had

had its effect, the couples began discussing those areas in their relationship. They were being videotaped. Men who received the oxytocin exhibited a more favourable response, and paid more attention to their partners than those that received the placebo. Physically their levels of emotional arousal increased, which researchers tracked by measuring their saliva for a chemical that is linked to the autonomous nervous system, which is responsible for generating emotions like happiness, anger, and flight or fight responses. The oxytocin made the women in the study more approachable and friendly towards their partners.

Increase your oxytocin levels by adopting the following:

- Be compassionate towards others
- Eat chocolate or any other comfort foods
- Have a lot of great sex with your partner
- Caress, touch, hug your partner or a friend or your kids
- Have a party with your closest friends
- Meditate
- Get a massage
- Get a dog or any pet
- Have a feeling of gratitude everyday for everything in your life
- Trust people and your partner
- Be emotionally intimate with your partner or a friend

If it's not in your bed, it's in your head

Serotonin, dopamine, and norepinephrine are also mood stabilizers. So if you are low on serotonin, you could get moody, sad, suffer from low self-esteem, low energy, be a bit confused, and have a sense of worthlessness. Just the opposite is true if you have healthy doses of serotonin. Low levels of dopamine can produce lethargy, weakness, and an excess of it can lead to anxiety and fear, while healthy levels of it will promote strength, vitality, and energy. Norepinephrine will produce the same negative effects as dopamine and healthy doses of it will give you strong flight and flight responses. So it's absolutely essential that you manage your neurotransmitters via food and lifestyle, as both these variables feed them.

Pheromones

Pheromones are chemical messengers that send signals to the opposite sex. In plants, insects, and animals they have many purposes, including marking food trails, and sending out an alarm (non verbal) that you are ready to mate or initiating mating. Sex pheromones can indicate attraction, interest, or mating readiness in some species. Our sense of smell is fundamental when it comes to our sex life. It's something that accompanies all aspects of your relationship—your first meeting, first impressions, and any conclusions you can draw about a potential partner. One of my boyfriends said to me that the first thing that hit him when he met me was my innate scent even before he was really attracted to me. After I started dating him, he'd insist I didn't wash my hair (sounds silly I know, and you are probably going yuck!) but that's how my pheromones affected him. I didn't really understand the impact of them till I met him. He probably had dog filters in his nose, because even if I entered the main door and he was upstairs in the house, he'd know I had come just by my smell.

As smells register in the hypothalamus, which is a primitive part of your brain, smells override any sort of 'rational' approach you might have to deciding whether someone is attractive or not. If a person doesn't smell good, you may have a hard time convincing yourself to be with them, no matter how good looking they are. One of my male friends recently remarked that if he went on a date and the woman did not smell good, he would be turned off no matter how good looking she was.

In the animal world, sex pheromones signal when a female is 'in heat' or is ready to mate. In the human world, they have much the same effect. Another interesting thing about smells is that women seem to be attracted to men who smell 'different' from the woman's family members. A research shows that when a woman smells the sweaty T-shirt of several men, she prefers the T-shirt of those men whose genetic make-up is unlike her own.[9] This could be due to the fact that she is protecting herself against inbreeding. Women in the study did not see these men, so the attraction was judged on smell alone.

Women usually think that perfumes and deodorants are enough to attract men, as do men when it comes to attracting women. However, your innate smell is actually sending stronger signals to your mate. Perfumes and deodorants only aid in masking this scent. In essence 'you are what you eat'. Ever eaten raw garlic, fenugreek, or drank copious amounts of alcohol to only then smelling like the food or drink you have consumed? That exactly proves the point. For eg., eating a lot of meat changes the way you smell. A Czech Republic research was conducted in 2006 to study the effect of red meat consumption on body odour attractiveness.[10] The vegetarians scored better in their smells than the non-vegetarians. High intake of animal fats affects the activity of the sweat and sebaceous glands in the skin. The free radical damage that also goes on in the body (free radicals are essential fatty acids which, when broken

---

[9] Claus Wedekind. 'The Sweaty T-Shirt Study' (1995)

[10] J. Havlicek and P. Lenochova. 'The effect of Meat Consumption on Body Odour Attractiveness,' Chemical Senses (2006) October 31st 31(8) 747-52

down, harm the body and cellular structure causing oxidative stress) causes these glands to get constricted. These saturated fats accumulate in the sweat ducts. Also a lifetime of poor eating habits like excessive animal food consumption, bad food combinations, excessive sugar, and dairy causes halitosis or bad breath, as your digestive lining is housing copious amounts of candida which sends this putrid smell into your mouth as well. Sticking to an alkaline diet—foods that do not cause the blood condition to get acidic, in that, more natural, wholesome, plant-based foods—and keeping the blood condition clean (strong pH balance) makes you send out the right pheromones while attracting a potential mate. More about how you can eat the right foods to attract a mate through pheromones in the next chapter.

Chasing the big O—the pursuit of the orgasm

Marnia Robinson in her book *Peace Between the Sheets* enumerates one of the major reasons there is disharmony between couples. She highlights how the trouble in relationships begins when partners become lovers. The difference is not exciting versus boring sex, but rather sex in itself and when couples start 'chasing the orgasm'. She advises couples to take the 'middle-path' i.e., the approach of making love continuously and frequently, without worrying about an orgasm. This has been practised for ages by the ancient sages, Taoists, and in the Ayurvedic tradition. Robinson goes on to discuss the *Coolidge Effect*. Scientists have found out that if you sexually exhaust a male rat with one female, his body chemistry will shut him down. If he were a guy, he would head for the recliner with a remote in hand. As a result of his changed body chemistry, namely fatigue, Miss Rat will look totally uninteresting to him. However, if he is near

Miss Ratty (a new female), his exhaustion will mysteriously fade long enough for him to gallantly fulfil his fertilization duties. This is known as the Coolidge Effect. The woman, in order to keep her man more excited, must use the strategy of holding out, not sexually exhaust her partner in the quest of an orgasm. Holding off the orgasm builds up to the Coolidge Effect.

New research in brain science (neuroendocrinology) proposes that emotional alienation between lovers may have less to do with communication or compatibility and more to do with a section of our brains called the pleasure/reward centre. Evolutionary biology currently exploits this brain mechanism by ensuring that we receive a powerful neurochemical 'reward' when we engage in sex (namely orgasm). That pay-off feels as though it is promoting bonding at the moment of orgasm, but the blasts trigger further neurochemical changes that, over time, push us apart from our lovers.

Here is how that works: the anticipation of an orgasm is due to a surge of dopamine; however the more satisfying reward is a cocktail of endorphins, which are further enhanced by the onset of oxytocin. You have heard many women say that most men just roll over and start snoring after the deed is done. We women feel let down when a man does not give us a cuddle or at least hold us after the whole act of making love is over. However, don't blame him; he is operating under the influence of the hormone prolactin. At climax, dopamine begins to shut down. Its goal of encouraging a fertilization attempt is over. Dopamine, however, has been holding back prolactin, mainly thought as a hormone that surges post pregnancy to promote lactation in women to breast feed. When prolactin rises after orgasm, it acts a sexual satiation mechanism, and distances you from your partner. The duration of how long this effect will last is really not known. People who can have multiple orgasms do not suffer from excess prolactin levels. High prolactin levels lead to headaches, menstrual issues, and make you feel low, and anxious, and usually women who are severely stressed go through this very often and also switch off sex. The good news is that we can continue to keep making love without getting distanced from our partners by sometimes holding off the orgasm *intentionally.*

Marnia advises to nurture our partners and not being selfish about our orgasms to encourage higher oxytocin levels. She says the gains from this are improved harmony between couples, and a healthier and longer life.

So if you want to add colour to your sex life, try holding off the orgasm, and not having sex for a while. Many sex therapies start by bringing your energy to touch, kissing, cuddling, and not to your genitals. Remember the time that you and your partner were not allowed to have sex, and back off sex for a while. This in turn will build the 'oxytocin effect'.

Sex and great sex

Helen E. Fisher talks about distinct neural pathways that are involved when romantic love happens, which led her to believe that romantic love is not an emotion.[11] Romantic love is basically a 'motivation system'. She says it's a mating drive that evolved millions of years ago. This drive is more powerful than the sex drive. You don't kill yourself when you don't get sex, but people kill themselves when they are parted from a lover. She concludes that sex drive evolved to get us out there looking for a mate; romantic love helped human beings focus on one mate at a time conserving mating time and energies; and attachment enabled human beings to tolerate this one person long enough to raise children with them.

---

[11] Helen Fisher. *Anatomy of Love: A Natural History of Mating, Marriage and Why we Stray.* Ballantine Books (1994).

10 things great sex does for you

1. Creates love
2. Is physically and emotionally satisfying
3. Heightens pleasure
4. When committed as casual sex, it may be a one-way street depleting energy; when its committed and long-term, you get the energy back
5. Is selfless and mutual
6. Is energizing and also energy-balancing
7. Is in the here and now, both partners are present to each other and need to engage
8. Involves the heart, and is a total mind, body, soul experience
9. Is communicating, expression need not be in words
10. Is meaningful

By having good sex, you have a yardstick of avoiding the bad sex defined by me as sex that leaves you feeling empty, depressed, and sad or sex that is disconnected and does not have any emotion, sex with an inappropriate partner, sex that is mechanical, or using sex just to have an orgasm, sex that only focuses on performance, or sex that is rushed and may leave you feeling not only dissatisfied but alienate you even further from your partner. It's a waste of time, and will leave you feeling more drained than vitalized, so my advice to you is don't engage in it.

Sex releases endorphins, also referred to as endogenous morphine (like an opiate), which are peptides that function also as neurotransmitters. Ever heard anyone tell you they had a great workout? That's because they have had all these endorphins release in their system, which gives them a high. Again produced in the pituitary gland and the spinal cord, they are also released during sex, when eating spicy food, when you are in love, when you get excited or are in pain, or when you are having an orgasm. They interact with receptors in cells found in regions of the brain known to *block pain* (also called pain killing hormones) and control emotion; therefore endorphins impact anyone prone to depression positively. Having sex is like getting a good workout, meditation, or the kind of high you feel after running—it releases endorphins which promote a feeling of well-being. A precursor to endorphins being released is a healthy dose of oxytocin. They take you to a level anywhere between being happy to a state of euphoria.

Check if you are suffering from any of these symptoms to see if you are running low on endorphins:

- Are grieving
- People call you overtly-sensitive
- Indulge in emotional eating
- Do not have the resilience to bounce back from a tough situation
- Feel sad sometimes for no apparent reason
- Cry at the drop of a hat
- Are a hypochondriac
- Have to make effort to be happy
- Have recently undergone trauma
- Are taking constant pain medication

Conventional Sex	Healing Sex
Impulsive, spur of the moment lovemaking	Gradual, conscious preparation priot to making love
Rapid movement	Emphasis on stillness
Tension	Relaxation

Urgent need for release	No need for release
Rapid conclusion	Prolonged union of cycles, erection comes and goes
Urgency to achieve a goal	Playfulness, ease in staying in the present, never hurried
Feelings of 'I want', 'I must have', or hunger	Can make love with enthusiasm or defer without disappointment
Sex is just sex	Sex is a delicious experience of companionship and comfort
Sense that partner is trying to control you, 'move too fast', or will abandon you	Sense of gratitude for the time spent together, you feel fortunate
Avoidance of closer union—due to projection of sense of deprivation or uneasiness onto partner	Desire for closer union—due to projection of increasing sense of well-being onto partner

by Marnia Robinson

Sex, stress, and your 'ki'

Quite literally your 'ki' is your key to unlocking doors of ecstasy in the bedroom. A healthy and vitalized 'ki' is essential for you to make it not only in the bedroom, but in life. Not wanting sex can be traced back to stress in your life which adds to stagnated ki.

Manisha, an investment banker, came to me complaining of no sex drive. She had trouble getting into the mood, and was far from achieving an orgasm every time she had sex. She suffered from dry vaginal syndrome which meant there was no lubrication when she had intercourse. She had been happily married for 6 years with no kids and she and her husband shared a loving relationship. Her sex life was affecting her relationship with her husband. Though they cared and loved each other, she felt that something was wrong with her.

Manisha had colitis, migraine, and was severely stressed out. She complained of sore tendons and muscles and aching bones. Her hormones were also out of whack as her blood tests indicated. Sexual response is greatly dependent on the hormones and how they perform—both sexual arousal and performance. She multi-tasked all the time. She set high standards for herself and was a type A personality: driven and an over-achiever. Stressed because of her work, and immersed in it with little room for her husband. Her diet was full of stimulants (as her adrenals were burnt out)—she consumed sugar all through the day in some form or the other, diet coke daily, coffee, tea, sweets, and a lot of white processed flour. With only one home-cooked meal daily, 80 percent of her day was spent eating junk. I classified her as being completely 'nutritionally deficient'.

While I recognized the adrenal fatigue immediately, she also had a lot of anxiety and worry stacked around her life, and the organs that are governed by these two emotions are the spleen, stomach, and pancreas. That was the reason behind the colitis—her stomach was off. Her ki energy was stuck in her gut. She was clearly, as I summed it up for her, *stagnated* with her ki energy. Also she was yin deficient, which was shown through her symptoms of vaginal dryness. Yin produces fluid in the body, while yang dries it up. Her diet was clearly full of drying foods.

With the right dietary and lifestyle changes, she recovered very well. I realized that she needed all her neurotransmitters coming out of her food. My diet for her included a simple whole grain, leafy greens, and beans; cutting out sugar, tea, coffee, and colas (which were adding to her vaginal dryness); and introducing some herbs. When the hormones are off, it always helps to do some yoga inversions as recommended in the exercise section—this moves ki to the right places to correct the balance.

Stress has a lot to do with your libido. It activates a chain reaction which affects your hormones which in turn suppresses libido. A person who is stressed out usually suffers from low energy levels and if complicated by a health issue, then it's a perfect combination for problems in the bedroom. In stressed women, estrogen raises a protein called sex hormone binding globulin (SHBG) which binds with testosterone in the cells, leaving women less aggressive in their response to stress as opposed to men who exhibit the fight or flight syndrome, but also leaving the body with lesser testosterone for libido. Sometimes stress can throw a woman's testosterone levels off resulting in acne, facial and body hair, and irritability.

Men on the other hand respond differently when confronted with stress in their environment, adopting the fight or flight strategy. This shoots up cortisol (hormone) levels, adrenaline, and norepinephrine (neurotransmitter). This affects testosterone as well as male libido by reducing the body's capacity of the pre-hormone compounds that are precursors to good testosterone production.

When the body is under stress, cortisol levels increase. Cortisol's primary function is to increase blood sugar and aid in fat, protein, and carbohydrate metabolism. When I say you are suffering from adrenal fatigue, it also means that cortisol levels, produced by the adrenal glands, in your body are high, causing imbalances. An excess of this hormone will send your blood sugar levels out of whack, making you gain weight. Also, high cortison levels cause a pre-disposition to having an impaired thyroid, high blood pressure, lower immunity, and negatively affect sex drive.

In the *Cortisol Connection*, author Shawn Talbott writes that elevated cortisol inhibits pre-hormone compounds that serve as precursors to testosterone production.[12] This also interferes with the normal response of the testicles to testosterone. Blood circulation goes to the extremities (arms and legs), cutting it off in the private areas. While endorphins, those wonderful chemicals produced during exercise, give you a 'runners high', an over production of endorphins result in suppressing testosterone by suppressing some hormonal steps required to produce it. Athletes who are involved in exercise of high endurance usually suffer from excess of cortisol and endorphins and suffer from low sperm count, sex drive, and lower testosterone. Too much cortisol can lead to being excitable, sleepless, and also make you prone to some psychosis. It definitely affects the libido.

In women, the menstrual cycle is divided into two distinct phases—the follicular phase where estrogen is the predominant hormone (and many other hormones) and ovulation (the release of an egg from the ovaries) which is the main event. The second phase of the menstrual cycle, known as the luteal phase, is dominated by progesterone, which stimulates the uterus to get ready for the egg to be implanted. Failing this you have a period, wherein the thickened uterine lining is discharged. When a woman is stressed, this whole process goes out of balance, estrogen and progesterone levels drop (or estrogen remains high, while progesterone levels drop), eggs are not released

---

[12] Shawn Talbott. *The Cortisol Connection: Why Stress Makes you Fat and Ruins Your Health-And What You Can do About It.* Publishers Group West, 2002.

from the body (anovulation), also affecting libido. Menstrual cycles get irregular (oligomenorrhea), and periods may also stop (amenorrhea). The same can be noted in female athletes who suffer from low estrogen and progesterone, impacting their menstrual cycles and leading to reduced sex drive or libido. The demands of their exercise regimens and diets put the body in a stress mode impacting these hormones.

Men can manifest stresses in a different way than women—premature ejaculation, taking a long time to ejaculate, and erectile dysfunction are some manifestations. Mihir and his wife were having trouble conceiving. He mentioned it quite openly to me that he was suffering from premature ejaculation. Anita, his wife, said that off late he had become irritable and short-tempered. The added pressure of conceiving a baby only added to his stress.

I first made Mihir address his stress—what he needed to do was not look at having a baby as a chore, but to get more involved with Anita in this process. He needed to look at sex as being a more fulfilling experience rather than just a routine, mechanical act. My advice to both was to get some exercise, apart from addressing dietary issues. This would improve circulation, delaying orgasm. These practices really helped him and in a few weeks he reported back to me saying he felt much better, and was able to delay his ejaculation. He was also able to connect more intimately with Anita. Most people don't want to admit that something maybe wrong with them sexually. The important part is to first admit it to yourself.

The basis of Macrobiotic diagnosis is rooted in Traditional Chinese Medicine (TCM) and in the beginning of the book I mentioned that the premise of having love in your life on any level is working with your 'ki' energy, cleaning up your life force, so your chakras a spinning efficiently and your nadis, or meridians, connecting to chakras are not blocked. For this free flow of ki, you need to be doing the following:

1. Not be stressed
2. Not eat food which will sludge up your liver namely fatty foods
3. Not harbour too many unfulfilled desires or dreams
4. Exercise
5. Not have unresolved anger and frustration
6. Not harbour grudges and resentments
7. Not be burdened by any negative sexual experiences
8. Not be overweight
9. Not be sad or depressed
10. Have abundant energy
11. Not consume excessive amounts of caffeine, tea, or stimulants like alcohol
12. Eat right to spice up your sex life, and choose foods that move the 'ki' and not stagnate it
13. Relax, and manage your stress levels
14. Take vitamin B for additional zinc to calm you down and magnesium to relax muscles
15. Get regular massages to unleash your stuck 'ki'
16. Consider bodywork therapies like acupuncture, acupressure, craniosacral therapy, polarity (chakra balancing), and shiatsu massage

Sexual energy is in itself a manifestation of ki; if you have healthy sexual appetite, you have strong ki.

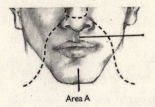

Area A

(Face Diagram: Analyse where you stand on your love quotient)

The area under the mount (chin) shows the condition of your sexual vitality. A healthy colour like a pinkish red signifies good sexual energy and vitality. What you are looking for is no marks, discolouration, or spots. Also, the colour of the area, in that is there enough blood circulation? Does it feel spongy on touch, or lifeless and depleted? If one has a cleft, it signifies very good sexual vitality. The length of the area between the nose and the start of your mouth (the mid area) signifies sexual appetite, the larger the width between the two, the larger the sexual appetite. You would also be looking for how pronounced the area is. Is it well defined? If you have both the width between the nose and upper lip, and the cleft, it is a sign of excellent sexual appetite and vitality.

Identify how strong your ki is: The great sex questionnaire

1. I suffer from constipation or diarrhea
2. My bones and joints hurt a lot sometimes

3. My extremities, i.e., hand and feet, are cold all the time
4. I suffer from muscle soreness
5. I am mostly angry towards my partner
6. I am more upset than happy in my life
7. When I am stressed, I can't think straight
8. I am frustrated
9. I have trouble achieving an orgasm
10. I am not interested in sex
11. I always have dark circles around my eyes
12. I suffer from asthma and allergies
13. I have trouble concentrating on one task for too long
14. I have no energy at the end of my work day
15. I keep things in and do not communicate them to my partner
16. I suffer from migraines
17. I find it difficult to relax when I take time off
18. I fly long distance more than once a month
19. I suffer from insomnia
20. I suffer from varicose veins
21. I get palpitations often
22. I tend to add a lot of salt to my food
23. I smoke more than 5 cigarettes daily
24. I am on a lot of medication
25. I have indulged in recreational drugs for a number of years
26. I am short of breath when I climb a flight of stairs

Women only

1. I have fibroids and/or polycystic ovaries
2. I sometimes skip my period

3. I suffer from extreme PMS (irritability, breast soreness)
4. I am in a lot of pain when I get my period
5. I am going through menopause and am in physical discomfort
6. I have excessive growth of body hair and/or facial hair
7. I am on thyroid medication
8. I have gone through fertility treatment
9. I am on the contraceptive pill
10. I have breast implants

Men only

1. I suffer from erectile dysfunction
2. I suffer from premature ejaculation
3. I take a long time to ejaculate
4. I have a receding hairline
5. My weight is concentrated largely around my abdomen
6. I am currently on antidepressants and medication for hypertension
7. I have suddenly gone grey in the last one year
8. I have a lower sex drive than I use to earlier
9. I have had some unexplained weight gain in the last couple of years
10. I am on thyroid medication

If you have checked more than five statements above, then your ki is stagnated. Higher the number of statements checked, higher is the stagnation of your ki energy and the more predisposed you are to having lower libido and lower sexual vitality.

Yin and yang come up in different ways in the body, and I would like to draw you attention to how deficient yin and yang would manifest. Let's look at the tendencies of yin and yang below.

YIN TENDENCIES	YANG TENDENCIES
Moist	Dry
Light	Dark
Passive	Active
Quiet	Loud
Light	Heavy
Cool	Hot
Passive	Active
Fire	Water
Descending	Rising
Soft	Hard

Radha came to me saying she just did not have sex on her mind at all. She said that having sex caused her pain due to excessive dryness in her vagina (she is 40-years-old). She just did not feel sexy enough and was suffering from negative body image. Her hair and skin were dry and her nails were brittle. When I analysed her, I realized her body lacked good quality fats. She suffered from hot flashes—a clear sign her body was creating a lot of heat (yang). She was obviously perimenopausal, but was also extremely yin deficient. If you look at the chart above and simply apply the yin tendencies that were not present in Radha's body, even you could come up with the conclusion that she lacked sufficient yin. I, of course, have different methods which point to my diagnosis.

Yin and yang need to be in harmony and balance all the time. They are complimentary, interdependent, and connected. So while menopause is inevitable in women, one does not have to switch off sex after that. We first got all of Radha's hormonal tests done, she was focussed on being a giver in her relationship with her husband (a yang tendency), so I made her focus on receiving rather than giving. We changed her diet to yin boosting foods like good quality oils (specially flax, chia seeds, as Essential Fatty Acids (EFAs) will impact estrogen levels positively), leafy greens, vegetables, all berries, whole grains like millet, whole wheat and pseudo-grains like amaranth, seeds, and nuts. I also gave her a calcium and magnesium supplement to aid her to calm down and magnesium helps with circulation. I made her eat less protein, especially meats (as they would only heat her up more), and suppress estrogen further. We monitored her weight—Radha was underweight, so we had to make her get back to balance by coming back to her normal weight—avoided stimulants, insisted she had plenty of liquids and stayed hydrated (as being deficient in yin will cause you to dry up), and took her off cigarettes (dehydrates you further). She went for craniosacral therapy as suggested by me to balance these two yin and yang energies and her ki.

A lot of my overweight clients complain that they just can't lose weight as their metabolism has slowed down and that they are tired all the time. Many women and men going through a thyroid issue feel this way—always associated with deficient yang. I have noticed a pattern with the overweight lot as well, they seem addicted to cold icy stuff, are erratic in their diet and lifestyle, suffer from sugar cravings practically all the time, and are in a state of tiredness constantly. All this burns the adrenal glands out. No wonder their sex life gets affected due to extreme tiredness and lethargy and the lower extremities are always cold. Again the thyroid is the master gland controlling hormones, so there are hormonal issues at play. For women, deficient yang may show up as excessive vaginal discharge and heavy periods. Here is how women or men who exhibit yang tendencies should manage: lay of the stress; regularize mealtimes and sleep times; stay away from cold and iced foods (will deplete kidney energy and they are already low), warming foods are always good like stews and soups; try staying away from pressure, it could be as simple as not setting high standards for yourself; exercise; establish work and personal boundaries; and, of course, eat the right foods. It's good to get your tests done to see where you may be deficient in that is the estrogen suffering in women or is it in excess, is progesterone low and/or is testosterone also out of whack. Men suffer from low yang as they age, (actually both yin and yang deplete with age). In men it affects their erections. Overall deficient yang will show up in men as being tired, weight gain, feeling cold, loss of bladder control, craving cold foods, apart from erectile dysfunction. A word of caution for males who work out (exercise) a lot: a sudden spurt of growth hormones androgens and testosterone may actually negatively impact libido, so you might have days when you are sexually supercharged, and days when you are just cold.

Ask yourself which traits are predominantly you—after looking at the yin yang tendency chart on page 131. Also ask yourself, given what you have read so far, if there are some signs of imbalance (especially if you took the ki test). Balancing yourself is the only way to also achieve a good sexual life with your partner. After you do this, try and engage in the following:

1. Take complete responsibility for yourself, as only you can change yourself
2. If you need to do some tests to determine how badly off your hormones are, then do them

3. If you are extremely stressed, book yourself an appointment with a psychologist (see end of the book for references)
4. Read and study the diet chapter carefully to see how much you can incorporate in your day-to-day life; avoid stimulants like alcohol and coffee
5. Exercise, whatever it may be. You must make the time for this
6. Seek out yin to balance yang. So if you have a hectic life and are in a stressful situation at work (yang), balance that by doing yoga and not going to the gym (which is also yang)
7. Meditate and visualize positivity
8. Get a massage, relax, unwind, go for a dance class
9. Don't try to be perfect
10. Take calcium, magnesium, and zinc—calcium will help you cope with stress, magnesium will help relieve muscular tension, and zinc will calm you down

Food and diet: Is it you, your mate, or in your plate?

Today, when I look back at how I have lived my life, there is only one thing that I can say has made me a better, healthier, and happier person—my food. It has the ability to change you to the extent you cannot imagine. We really don't live to eat, but actually 'eat to live a better life'. The Buddha said, 'Eating is like a disease we are born with. It is something we must heal on a daily basis; otherwise, it will lead to other irritations like greed, hatred, delusion, attachment, envy, etc.'

Steve Gagne in his book *The Energetics of Food* talks about food as being the most intimate relationship you'll ever have in your life.[13] 'Food energetics' he says is the *true knowledge* foods impart to you when you eat them and experience them. Every food has its own character and personality. What you should be doing is getting to know your food's character and personality, just as you would get to *know* a new friend.

Michio Kushi in the book *The Macrobiotic Way* says in order to recover our physical, mental, and spiritual health, we need to reorient our way of life in the following ways:

- We should reflect upon our own daily life—whether we are pursuing only sensory pleasure and emotional comfort forgetting our native potential for greater happiness and higher freedom

- We should reflect further upon our daily food and drink and consider whether our meals are really balanced to produce the best quality of blood and cells as well as to secure the best mental and spiritual comditions

- We should also reflect upon our thought and behaviour toward our parents, family, friends and other people and consider whether our behaviour toward them is really serving for health and happiness

- We should also reflect upon our direction as a society and consider whether we are building cultures and civilizations in harmony with the order of nature or ignoring the natural environment

- We should reflect, finally, upon our understanding of the cosmos: do we really know where we have come from and where we are going in this infinite universe?

---

[13] Steve Gagne, *The Energetics of Food* (Healing Arts Press; 3 edition; 5 November 2008).

Through proper dietary habits, our blood, body, and mind will become sound and whole. Mental and spiritual well-being will follow naturally. Food is creating us every minute, every second. If the nourishment we receive is proper, we are naturally more energetic physically, more comfortable emotionally, and more elevated spiritually than when our way of eating in imbalanced and disorderly. Personal feelings, social relations, and our approach to any problems are influenced by the way we eat. Our physical and mental habits, as well as tendencies in our thinking and capacities of our consciousness, all depend upon what we have been eating for a long period—from the embryonic stage through childhood up to the present. To change our food is to wholly change ourselves. Through food, consciously or unconsciously, we shape our destiny and follow our dreams. So let's look at *The Love Diet* in that manner, break it up—take the parts that make for a better relationship with your partner, but also look at it towards changing yourself to be a better person.

The attraction of opposites is ubiquitous; yin and yang are evident in everyday life, in your response to your environment and your relationships. As explained in the first chapter, the same force that brings you together is also the force that makes the Earth rotate, the stars shine bright, and nature so bountiful. Sex is the physical exchange that results from the attraction of the sexes. It involves the chakra response, activating mind, body and spirit. When men and women communicate, they have a satisfying emotional relationship this is bound to manifest in sexuality between them as well. As Michio Kushi says, 'Without love, the goal of sex becomes only one-sided. It becomes a mechanical act devoid of emotion and spirituality. Creating the right kind of love also helps men and women to transcend their immediate desires and achieve harmony, and take sexuality to higher levels of psychic and spiritual interaction.' The most important ingredient for your vitality and sexual health is your diet.

Food is energy as well and has a yin and yang attached to it. All foods can be categorized according to the type of energy they carry. For example, eggs are condensed, compact, and have concentrated energy (yang) as compared to vegetables which have an expansive quality (yin) about them. The energy we receive from the foods we eat directly impact the energy in the chakras and the responses we have towards our partners in life and during sex. When men and women eat a lot of eggs, butter chicken, and meat, the accumulation of fat and cholesterol throughout the body may cause them to lose conductivity of the forces of heaven and earth, impacting their ki energy.

Foods	Yin/Yang
Meats	Yang
Eggs	Yang
Chicken	Yang
Cheese	Yang
Saturated Fat	Yang
Salt	Yang
Vegetables	Balanced
Sugar	Yin
Spices	Yin
Coffee/Tea	Yin
Medications	Yin
Fruits	Yin
Chocolate	Yin

Foods	Yin/Yang
Alcohol	Yin
Dairy	Yin
Honey	Yin
Oil	Yin
Nuts	Yin/Yang
Fish	Yin/Yang
Beans	Balanced
Whole Grain	Balanced

So, while animals may survive on plant foods, they themselves are full of saturated fat, sodium (salts as preservatives), protein, and in the case of dairy—calcium and minerals. These are more yang. They are charged with contractive energy and balance must be sought from the plant kingdom, if one is to eat meat/chicken and dairy products. When these are consumed in excess, stagnated 'ki' energy is produced in the form of fatty deposits made up of saturated fat and cholesterol that will block arteries and nerve pathways, cutting off circulation to the body's organs and tissues. The influx of saturated fat from animal foods and dairy hardens the skin and organs—the leathery look that some people have is due to overconsumption of meats.

Sugar, too much fruit, coffee, chocolates, alcohol, and medication have expansive effects on the mind and the body. You must have heard phrases like 'on a coffee or sugar high'. These foods generate quick bursts of energy, and simple sugars (honey, refined sugar, processed and refined white flours) will always make your blood sugar levels crash, after first going up, post consuming them, further causing mood swings, energy lows, and cravings. Plant foods (what we Indians term as vegetarian foods) cause balanced yin energy. Whole grains bring in steady supply of sugars for normal brain activity and an infusion of vitality.

Your blood has a pH—potential of hydrogen which is a measure of the acidity or alkalinity of your blood—balance to it. You can swing between being acidic and or being alkaline. An excess of both is not good for the body. The foods that don't assimilate and make for bad blood, veer too much towards acidic. What you need to be is closer to neutral, where your pH is close to 7 (on a scale designed to facilitate reading of your blood being acid or alkaline). If you are too acidic, you pH will slow down your body's ability to retain energy which will impact your vitality in sustaining a healthy relationship with your partner. Being too alkaline can cause you to be very weak, again impacting energy levels. It's important to know pH triggers which are listed below:

- Dairy products
- Animal food
- Sugar (including honey and sweeteners)
- Refined and processed flours
- Refined and processed foods
- Canned foods, frozen foods
- Alcohol
- Colas, sodas, and aerated beverages
- Coffee and tea (except herbal or green tea)
- Refined oils
- Yeasted products
- Stress

This basically means that if you consume these in excess, there is a good chance that your pH is off. However, it can be restored with a healthy diet and an infusion of good probiotics (good bacteria), mainly through food. Inflammation is defined as the body's short-term response to any issues that your immune system is suffering from—this could be a reaction of your immune system to some trauma (like a pH that is off), an injury, toxic lifestyle, or excessive medication. Your body will show inflammation in different ways, like discharges from the body which could range from skin disorders, allergies, arthritis, swelling in the body or pain, autoimmune disorders, high blood pressure, diabetes, colitis, irritable bowel disorder (IBD), or asthma. A test called the C-reactive protein test will measure the hidden inflammation in your body. I speak of this because almost every major illness is a result of inflammation in the body. We need to first identify the cause of the inflammation and then use the corrective diet to treat it—for eg. sometimes a simple thing like gluten (contained in wheat) could be a cause. You may be lactose intolerant and not know about it, or there may be a hair or skin product you are using which does not suit you; therefore isolating the reason for inflammation is very important. The tools outlined in this book are meant to tackle the inflammation you have.

The basics of love and food

Your skin response and love

Your circulatory system comprises of capillaries, main arteries, and veins, and the organ that runs over all of this is your skin. Your skin is the largest breathing organ, and is discharging toxins—which have not been assimilated from you food—all the time. Animal foods, refined oils, and dairy that bring in saturated fats and cholesterol, apart from restricting blood vessels as mentioned above and stagnating your ki, make your skin rigid and inflexible. The skin's collagen is a protein which keeps your skin together giving it that firmness and plumpness. Collagen is the main component of the connective tissue of the body. 80 percent of the portion under the top layer of the skin (epidermis) is made up of collagen. Elastin (as elasticity) give your skin the strength to be resilient—in other words, bounce back. Both saturated fat and cholesterol cause the ratio of collagen and elastin to shift and deplete elastin and raising collagen which makes the skin hard—that leathery feeling skin. 71 percent of the collagen is of the insoluble variety and forms tissues that connect tendons, bones, and internal organs. An overconsumption of fats will change the soluble collagen to insoluble collagen, by depositing free radicals (breakdown of fats having negative charge) within the collagen fibres. This produces a hardening of the skin and the loss of natural oils and moisture producing dry skin. The skin also is a conductor of the heaven's and earth's energy (force) travelling along the meridians (nadis) to the chakras. There is an inflow and outflow of this energy from the chakras as well. Sexuality is affected by the smooth inflow and outflow of this energy. If you are overburdened with this fat, you may also experience a cutting away from your environment and people, manifesting in you being self-absorbed, thus affecting your interpersonal relationship with your partner. Your skin will eventually also receive less blood due to the circulatory systems being affected, including oxygen which revitalizes the cells, accelerating the ageing process and the speed up of menopause and manopause (andropause or hypogonadism is defined as decreased testosterone production in men as they age). The skin no longer eliminates toxins as it should, leave alone being sensitive to touch and any sensory experience as part of the sexuality between the sexes. In men, the consumption of foods high in saturated fat will affect their prostate gland and decrease blood supply to the sexual organs. Foods like lard, cheese, butter, and dairy products will add to hardening of tissue around the prostate, causing cancers and other complications. An enlargement of the prostate is aggravated by the consumption of yin foods like sugars, alcohol, simple sugars, coffee, and excessive medication. During sex, the prostate contracts (for an erection to take place) and an enlarged prostate may not actually contract the way it should, affecting erection and orgasm in men.

In women, the tissues of the vagina get affected and the sensitivity in this area will lessen, affecting vaginal lubrication. This fluid conducts the exchange between men and women during sex. This will decrease the amount of pleasure a woman will derive from sex, interfering with the orgasmic process.

BODY SCRUBS

One way of increasing you skin's response to love and eliminating toxins is to do a body scrub daily. This could be done either before soaping yourself or after. Take a cotton face towel (in fact, keep 4 of them aside just for your body scrubs) and wet it with warm water (as hot as you can bear). Pick an area of your body e.g., one arm and scrub it (the pressure should be such that the skin turns red). Now repeat this process with another area, after wetting the wash cloth again. Scrub yourself all over: legs, thighs, buttocks, behind the ears, especially behind each joint, as maximum discharge collects in these areas, under the soles of your foot, back, chest, sides of the body. Not only will you activate blood circulation, but body scrubs will promote mental and physical energy in the body as well.

Stress, fatigue, and foods

In similar vein, a diet rich in meats, eggs, and other animal foods will cause a tightening of the body's muscles, adding to stress. It can make you rigid and inflexible and often unable to relax. A diet where there is too much of sugars, alcohol, fruit sugars, spices, and simple sugars will make you feel scattered and therefore unable to focus and concentrate on the needs of your partner.

Apart from life demanding vitality, sex also demands the same vitality and in abundance. Sexual performance enhancers, stimulants, etc. are touted to up your vitality by marketers when in reality there is no real need for them if you are eating healthy. The adrenal fatigue I mentioned in the earlier chapters impacts all of us today and in unimaginable ways. Low blood sugar or hypoglycaemia is a big factor that prolongs adrenal fatigue. Pancreas is your regulator of insulin (sugars) in the blood. The accumulation of hard fats makes this organ tensed. So if someone is prone to eating more sugars (yin), the blood sugar rises and insulin is released in large doses in the system. The opposite occurs when animal fats, salts, and proteins are consumed, a low blood sugar level response occurs. When the pancreas become tense, they are unable to secrete anti-insulin—this keeps blood sugar levels high at first and then a crash happens, i.e. low blood sugars within the body, causing hypoglycaemia. This condition brings with its own hosts of issues like anxiety, depression, and a lot of fatigue. This also causes cravings leading to the munchies usually accompanied with more sugar. The impact of this yo-yo situation will affect you and your partner. Along with anxiety, your self-image, self-confidence, and body image will all be hit under this pseudo-influence of blood sugars in your system. Sugars will also leach minerals and impact your energy and vitality—magnesium which relaxes muscles will get depleted or zinc which calms you down will be impacted.

Whole grains which have complex sugars are broken down slowly in the body, thereby entering the blood stream in an orderly manner. The liver stores glycogen, i.e, sugars until it can be converted to glucose, and an excess of what is stored here gets dumped into the blood in the form of fatty acids and collects in your thighs, buttocks, breasts, and waist area.If there is an excess of sugars consumed, then it builds up in your kidneys, prostate, ovaries, and heart, which gets loaded with thick mucous.

As this mucous gets lodged in tissues of the organs, their functioning is impaired, resulting in lethargy, fatigue, and a decreased desire for sex. The chakras are thermal in nature. If you are in a yang—contracted, dried up, overtly acidic—state, then the tendency will be to gravitate towards iced cold drinks and foods. This will cool the chakra energy down, and impair energy flow here. The kidneys, which are also attached to adrenals, burn out with cold foods.

Manopause: According to their book *Manopause Your Guide to Surviving His Changing Life*, authors Lisa Friedman Bloch and Kathy Kirtland Silverman say that the changes men go through at mid-life are the same as those encountered by a woman when she goes through menopause. It is accompanied by hormonal loss, physical changes, and also what the society expects a man to be. This also could result in behaviours such as irritability, mood swings, hypersensitivity, and a bit of depression.

Love food

The balanced foods are whole grains, vegetables, and beans. These foods are not on the extreme end of the yin and yang polarities and have the same effect on stabilizing your sexual energies. Mind you, I am not negating the non-vegetarian diet here, but you need to balance this out and seek a more plant-based approach. The more balanced foods have complex carbohydrates (compact sugar molecules) further broken down by chewing sustained sugars which are released in the system, therefore they provide sustained energy. They also comprise of fats, minerals, proteins, and fibre, supplying you with physical endurance for your love life. Simple sugars give you that quick burst of energy with a low called the 'sugar blues' and this will impact energy negatively. A diet that will bring in peak performance (pun intended) is the one that will avoid saturated fats (meats and dairy), sugars that are refined, and stimulants (alcohol, coffees, teas, medications, drugs). Minerals are lacking in the Indian diet and should be pulled in from sea salt or rock salt and spirulina—the only sea vegetable available at the moment—besides kombu that is available in speciality stores.

In a quick summary, you need to do the following to get your love diet right:

- A higher consumption of complex carbohydrates and reducing the intake of simple sugars
- A lower intake of fat by increasing the use of unsaturated fats and oils and decreasing saturated fats
- Using more protein from whole grains, beans, and other vegetables by combining a balanced meal plan and relying on animal proteins less, except fish
- The right balance of minerals and vitamins

- Using traditional and local foods and less of processed and refined foods
- Using foods that are left whole, rather than those that have been refined
- Using antioxidants that promote health and vitality
- Using aphrodisiacs as supplements via foods

Let's break down the elements of love

'May God give you of the dew of heaven and of the fatness of the earth and plenty of grain and wine.'

THE BOOK OF GENESIS

Grains: The first element we're going to discuss is grains. In an earlier section, I explained the spiral of creation and ratio of 1:7 that manifests in nature. To quickly recap, heaven's downward force is seven times stronger than earth's expanding energy and the food that represents this ratio perfectly is whole cereal grain. Cereal grains are associated with fertility, abundance, and fecundity. Among Hindus, when the bride enters the home, she first uses her right foot to knock down rice which symbolizes wealth and abundance. Similarly, rice is showered on couples, which symbolizes fertility in Catholic and Hindu weddings. Grain such as brown rice, millet, oats (whole), corn, wheat, and buckwheat (kuttu) contain ideal proportions of protein, minerals, and vitamins. Grains become the building blocks for sustained energy needed for sexual health and vitality.

The main roadblock for energy in most people who do not eat well and have long-term poor dietary habits is a build-up of stuck and stagnated ki in the digestive tract, and grains bring in the fibre to release this energy. Modern diet with its hosts of sugars, high fats, and low fibre causes the energy in the digestive system to get stuck, inhibiting the lower chakras as well. Grains too are yin and yang. If you want a more concentrated energy in the lower chakras and good blood flow, then special attention should be paid to yang grains like wheat, rye (closely related to barley), whole, nachni, and bajra. While yin grains like barley, fox tail millet, corn, and jowar activate the emotional responses and upper chakras, it's always best to have a combination of both in your diet. Grains also provide sustained serotonin, as they give you those sustained sugars. Brown rice is known to be a complete food for enhanced sexual drive—not only does it have all the B vitamins, it also has zinc, iron magnesium, chromium, and calcium.

Vegetables: For maximum vitality, it is better to include a range of vegetables in your diet. Round vegetables will affect lower chakras, heart, and middle regions of the body and have both expanding and contracting energies. Round vegetables also contribute to stabilizing blood sugar levels and help strengthen emotions while strengthening the heart chakra. Leafy greens vitalize the upper chakras and increase our receptivity to sensory experiences of touch and other stimulation. Root vegetables have a downward energy charge and an upward charge, so they affect all chakras. All starchy vegetables are known to provide serotonin as well.

In the vegetable group of food, there is a theory that those that are high on nitrogen compounds like leafy greens help with the production on Nitric Oxide (NO)—a neurotransmitter which helps blood vessels relax and improves circulation, which has a crucial impact on creating love between your partner and you. It is also known as herbal viagra, and is now being sold by vitamin shops over the counter in the West.

Nitric Oxide (NO) is a crucial factor in sexual arousal. To understand how we use food to keep our sexual organs vitalized, it is important to understand how they work first. Most people know very little about the way their sex organs work and very often it's this ignorance that is actually getting in the way of sexual satisfaction.

Cardiovascular function has a lot to do with being happy in the bedroom. When sexual arousal happens, blood flow to the sex organs increases as needed to flood the tissues of those organs. For men, this is experienced as an erection, and for women it is lubrication of the vaginal tissue.

The real benefits of NO were discovered by Dr Salvador Moncada who unmasked it as a gas. It is extracted from an amino acid L-arginine. Scientists soon connected it to lowering blood pressure, promoting heart function, lowering serum LDL cholesterol (bad cholesterol), and strengthening sexual function and vitality. Dr Robert Fried and Lynn Edlen-Nezin then connected the dots to establish the relationship between NO and foods.

At the centre of leafy green plant foods is chlorophyll. Blood which is made of haemoglobin is fuelled by this cholorophyll. Greens also are a ready supply of nitrogen compounds necessary to produce NO. Common greens in the Indian Subcontinent include amaranth (cholai), spinach (paalak which contains Co-Q10, iron, folic acid, beta carotene, vitamins B3, B6, and C, calcium and magnesium), fenugreek (methi), bok choy (not native to India but available), celery, asparagus, broccoli, green cabbage, cauliflower, cucumbers, lettuce, peas, alfalfa sprouts, and green beans (what we Indian call French beans).

While the Indian Subcontinent does not have too many sea vegetables to offer except spirulina which is now being harvested, this is an important vegetable group. Sea vegetables are known for opening up the mind, making you very focussed, as they provide all the necessary minerals which affect your nervous system positively. Sea vegetables carry a strong electromagnetic charge from the environment (*We came from the sea and we all go back to the sea. Our bodies are made of the same percentage of salt that exists in the oceans; this includes the molecular structure of our bodily fluids which is in the same ratio as the water of the oceans and seas—we are tied to the oceans as our innate environment.*) This charge resonates the most with our chakras and meridians. The other one that is now being sold in India is called kombu (however this is not available widely and only in some specialty stores) Also rich in arginine, an amino acid, sea vegetables are ready sources of NO and chlorophyll.

Beans: The other food group which is also rich in nitrogen compound are beans—the third element on the love diet plan. Beans are rich in phthalides (a compound known to give aroma and flavour to celery—also stimulates the pituitary gland that produce the sex hormones) known to relax arteries and saponin (phytochemicals). Both phthalides and saponin lower serum cholesterol. Saponins are also antioxidant in nature and are known to stimulate the immune system. Beans are also high in folic acid, vitamin B6, B12, E and C, flavonoids, and phytoestrogens, which help lower homocysteine and serum cholesterol. K.S. McCully (in the book *The Homocysteine Revolution*, 1996) also linked homocysteine an amino acid, a by-product of the protein metabolism, which causes damage to arterial blood vessels as it ends up forming LDl cholesterol deposits. If your diet is rich in B12, B6, and folic acid, these effects can be mitigated. Apart from all this, beans are rich in protein and are precursors for the production of dopamine as all foods rich in amino acids are.

A balanced meal of whole grains, beans, and vegetables provides us with the complete protein required by our body. All whole beans and lentils are in the Bean category of food, which forms the basis of the third element of creating the love you want. The complex carbohydrates in these beans provide the slow energy required by the body which infuses with the rapid energy given by the vegetables and peaceful energy given by the whole grains. This 'combustion' of energies helps with providing long-lasting energy required between partners for love to manifest and sustain itself. Beans add to the smooth functioning of the circulatory, digestive, and nervous systems in the human body. Beans, specially soybeans, kidney beans, black kidney and white kidney beans, chickpeas, and azuki (not available in India that easily) add to the optimum functioning of the adrenal glands and also the sexual organs. Soy beans in particular impact the blood vessels and circulatory system, as they are higher on protein and good fats. A word of caution with soy—soy milk is yin and expansive, (for example tofu is also yin), and if eaten in excess, will actually curb sexual desire.

Another discovery is that of arginine, an amino acid which helps with protein synthesis. Arginine is important in the creation of a healthy bond between your partner and you as it is the principal source of Nitric Oxide (NO). Dr Robert Fried and Dr Woodson C. Merrel talk about the benefits of this amino acid on blood circulation, blood pressure, heart health and plaque prevention, sexuality, and the immune system in their book *The Arginine Solution* (1999). Arginine from foods come from whole grains, sea foods, soy, legumes, red meat, spinach and leafy greens, nuts (which contain alpha linolenic acid (ALA), vitamin E, magnesium, copper and folic acid), seafood, vegetable protein sources, and eggs. One of the biggest superfoods is goji berries which are rich in arginine. There is a strong link established between arginine, NO, and sexuality. It was reported in *The International Journal of Impotence Research* in 1994 that oral arginine taken for two weeks significantly improves erectile function in impotent men.[14] Vegetarians who do not eat eggs and dairy products (vegans) could be at a risk for deficient arginine which is why including nuts, wheat, germ, legumes, and seeds are all essential in their case. In the same vein, a high carbohydrate, low fat, and high-protein diet may cause arginine deficiency.

You can rev up your love life with nuts—a good source of dietary fibre. Although most dieticians focussing on weight loss will take you off nuts, a report in 1999 called the Adventist Health Study said that those participants who frequently ate nuts were actually leaner than those who didn't eat nuts. In the Indian markets, apart from almonds (full of magnesium and EFAs required for the production of sex hormones, calcium, zinc, folic acid, Vitamins Bs and E), walnuts, pine nuts, coconut, peanuts, pistachios, we also get pecans which are very good for health. Among seeds, sunflower and pumpkin seeds are widely available.

Antioxidants: Antioxidants are another element considered to boost love in the quest to seek balance in the body. The foods we eat, if they don't assimilate, generate free radicals. Free radicals, if left to wander around in your body, cause issues with the cellular structure. Consider free radicals as the only things which will destroy your cells, leading to a low immune response and disease. Whether we are generating free radicals is also affected by other factors such as our levels of over-exercise, stress, food additives, alcohol in excess, exposure to radiation (like our manic obsession with cell phones in this age), and the environmental pollution we are exposed to. They can be very

---

[14] Zorgniotti, A. W., et al. 'Effect of the large doses of the Nitric oxide Precursor L-Arginine, on Erectile Dysfunction,' International Journal of Impotence Research, Vol 6 (1) March 1994 (33-35)

damaging to body tissues, accelerating ageing and impairing sexual health. Free radicals have the ability to latch onto cells and change the way they would normally behave for smooth functioning of the body. Oxidative stress is the term used to describe the damage that free radicals resulting from our body's metabolic processes have on our organs, tissues, and cellular structure. So antioxidant foods should form a large part of one's diet, not just for sexual health but general health and vitality. Antioxidants are also called free radical scavengers.

This is why cancers occur when the cell membranes get damaged. William Li, a doctor based in the US, came up with a theory called Angiogenesis wherein he looks at the body's ability to regulate blood vessels with stimulators and inhibitors. His study led him to discover a blend of anti-angiogenic drugs that inhibit the cancer cells to be fed with blood thus preventing the spread and growth of cancer cells. He has successfully treated 11 cancer types with 12 anti-angiogenic drugs. He came to the conclusion at the end of his study that Mother Nature, which provides us with plant based foods, has natural inhibitors to the process of angiogenesis. In essence, we get all our anti-angiogenic nutrients from our food alone. His study made him test resveratrol—a type of natural phenol in red wine—now called an antioxidant which inhibited cancer upto 60 percent or strawberries with ellagic acid, again a natural phenol antioxidant also found in cranberries, pomegranete, raspberries, walnuts, and grapes all inhibiting cancers and slowing down the damage caused by free radicals. He isolated the following list of foods that had high anti-angiogenic properties:

- Green tea
- Blueberries
- Red grapes

- Grapefruit
- Pineapple
- Lemons
- Apples
- Oranges
- Pineapple
- Ginseng
- Bok Choy
- Kale
- Soy beans
- Maitake mushrooms
- Licorice
- Turmeric
- Nutmeg
- Lavender
- Pumpkin
- Sea cucumber
- Tomatoes
- Olive oil
- Grapeseed oil
- Dark chocolate

> Men who consume 2–3 servings of cooked tomatoes per week have a reduced risk of developing prostate cancer by 40–50 percent according to Dr Lirelei Mucci of Harvard School of Public Health. Tomatoes have lycopene (a carotenoid responsible for giving tomatoes its red colour, also in watermelon, papaya, and guava) which is an antioxidant.

Free radicals are especially damaging to blood vessels because they can directly damage the endothelium and also cause blood pressure to rise. This damage is observed in blood vessels of the penis as well, and has been linked to erectile dysfunction. This is also a reason why antioxidants become an important part of the love diet.

Another positive affect that antioxidants have is on the levels of oxidized LDL cholesterol in postmenopausal women as they produce less estrogen. Estrogen actually helps women, in that, it promotes healthy functioning of the endolethium. A decline in estrogen will cause an increase in a substance called ADMA that inhibits the release of ENOS necessary to form NO.

Another set of antioxidants emerge from nutrient chemicals in plants called phytochemicals. Polyphenols are present in plant compounds, which give the flavour, colour, and taste to vegetables, fruits, and seeds. Like the lycopene in tomatoes or the phthalides in celery. They all have properties which are anti-ageing, and protect major organs of the body and make you stronger and healthier. Plants derive their immune system strength from polyphenols, so there's no reason why they will not make us strong too. Also plant lignans are biologically important class of phenolic compounds (impact estrogen positively), the richest source of such lignans are flax seeds, also rich in omega 3 fatty acids and high on fibre.

These are a few more antioxidants that you will need:

➢ Lycopene red cartenoid in tomatoes, papaya, and watermelons (also present in grapefruit which is pinkish red in colour)
➢ Lutein and zeaxanthin helps prevent eye degeneration found in dark green vegetables, broccoli, green and yellow peppers, corn, kinus, and goji berries (native to Tibet and China, known to enhance sexual drive)

- Proanthocyanidins in green veggies, red wine, and grape juice
- Resveratrol in red wine, red grapes, green tea, and cacao powder
- Flavonoids found in red wine, citrus fruits, and dark chocolate
- Lignans in flax seeds, sesame seeds, some whole grains (barley, wheat and whole oats), cruciferous vegetables like cauliflower and broccoli, and apricots, strawberries, and soybean
- Vitamin C found in tomatoes, citrus fruits, peppers, potatoes, broccoli, gooseberry (amla), lychee, and green chillies. Vitamin C increases semen volume and ensures that sperm don't bunch together. It boosts sex drive, making your sexual organs stronger
- Indole carbinol 3 in cruiceferous vegetables, cauliflower, cabbage, and broccoli
- Carotenoids, of which beta-carotene is the major one, found in pumpkin (lal kaddu or bhopla), carrots, goji berries, sweet potatoes, and yellow vegetables like yellow peppers or cantaloupe
- Beta-1, 3-D glucan found in whole oats (not rolled oats), barley, maitake mushrooms, more concentrated in the outer layers of any cereal grain, also referred to as bran
- Ellagic acid in strawberries, walnuts, apples, pomegranates, raspberries, and grapes
- Vitamin E found in wheat germ, sunflower, and safflower oils, avocados, asparagus, sweet potato, broccoli, nuts (of which almonds have the highest amount), the tops of turnips (shalgam), tomatoes, pine nuts (chilgoza—rich source of minerals, protein, zinc, magnesium (shrimp

is an excellent source of zinc and magnesium both), B vitamins, and calcium. The reason you see Vitamin E in the Indian market as a gel–like capsule (which has the oil) is because it is a fat-soluble vitamin and requires the fat to be absorbed in the body. It's great for your skin and pumps all that collagen and elastin needed for a natural touch

➢ Selenium is required in small quantities. It's a trace mineral from nuts, liver, sunflower seeds, fish, all grain brans, spirulina, shitake mushrooms, onions, goji berries, celery, sesame seeds, and fish. It has been known to increase sperm motility and impact male fertility positively. It also helps with the utilization of oxygen required for endurance and stamina

➢ Superoxide dismutase (SOD), catalase (CAT), and glutathione perioxidase (GPx) help in repairing oxidized DNA, oxidized protein, and oxidized lipids (fats). SOD foods include wheat grass, barley grass, broccoli, and cabbage; CAT foods include wheat sprouts, potatoes, and carrots; GPx is found in milk thistle (excellent for your liver), asparagus, broccoli, avocado, spinach, turmeric, and selenium which is a co-factor that helps synthesize GPx. Healthy bodies produce Alpha Lipoic Acid (ALA). It protects your cells as all other antioxidants do. Diabetics using insulin are advised not to take ALA. It is responsible for energy production; it actually works as a support acid to glutathione, vitamin C, and E when these wear themselves out by fighting those free radicals. ALA is found where lysine (amino acid) is bound to protein so essentially in meats, broccoli, spinach and brewer's yeast (a by-product of brewing beer; also known as baker's yeast)

➤ Coenzyme Q-10 found in wheat germ (or other germ portions of grains), fish, seeds, nuts, canola and soybean oils, broccoli, cauliflower, strawberries (which also have iron, beta carotene, folic acid, vitamin E, calcium, and magnesium), and oranges. Required for the small mitochondria (in cells) where we produce energy.

➤ Anthocyanins are red to blue pigments found in foods, more concentrated in black colour foods. Anthocyanins are found in berries like blueberries, cranberries, black and red raspberries, cherries, red cabbage, black soybean, and black grapes

Fruits that also are high in antioxidants and arginine are dates, mangoes, figs, apples, pears, peaches, plums, and pomegranates.

MYTH 1: SUPPLEMENTING WITH ANTIOXIDANTS POST YOUR WORKOUT IS A GOOD WAY TO ABSORB ANTIOXIDANTS

Not at all. If you're exercising to lose weight, your antioxidants should come from whole foods, not from supplements or antioxidant-enhanced food products. Working out not only leads to an increase in free radicals, but also more oxidation. Exercise leads to a positive natural physical and emotional response in your body. By adding antioxidants post your workout, you take away from the positives of this action.

So by all means drink your green tea, but you will need at least a litre daily to get the antioxidants that would help you. Make sure your diet is rich in whole grains, beans, vegetables, fruit, fish, nuts, and seeds, and don't indulge in antioxidant fortified processed foods as most processed foods have relatively small amounts of just one or two kinds of antioxidants, whereas a variety of antioxidants would work better for you.

MYTH 2: FREE RADICALS MUST BE DESTROYED

<u>Not necessarily</u>. Sometimes we actually need these free radicals. Free radicals are released when oxidation occurs in the body and are actually required as they defend your body. It's just that too many of them can cause harm. If you are doing your body harm with smoking, drinking, and bad dietary habits, by switching to a healthy eating routine, you can up the quotient of antioxidants which reduces the damage that can be caused by these free radicals floating around in your system.

I cannot stress enough the importance of zinc in your diet as it is strongly linked to fertility (normal sperm count) and the regulation of sex drive. The prostate has a concentration of zinc, and a healthy prostate in men is responsible for great sex, so a zinc deficiency could do you in. Zinc also helps with formation of enzymes that regulate your sense of smell and taste, which are important for sexual arousal. Shellfish and seafood, brown rice, legumes, pine nuts, peanuts, sesame and pumpkin seeds, cashews, peanut butter, spirulina, and eggs are rich in zinc.

Additional food elements: Fish is an excellent low-fat source of powerful protein and omega-3s and great polyunsaturated oils (PUFAs). Fish oils help in endothelial functioning, and enhance NO. While I am not advocating going off animal foods completely for the non-vegetarians, I do advocate achieving a balance with animal foods, chicken, eggs, and dairy—so moderation is the name of the game. Eat fruit, but not in excess, as the fructose from fruit enters the bloodstream swiftly raising energy levels. An excessive amount will actually deplete chakra energy. Nuts and seeds can also form a part of additional food factors.

I highly recommend coconut, and anything to do with them i.e. oil and milk of the coconut. Coconut oil is known to increase energy as it does not require bile for digestion, and the body turns the fatty acids into energy right away. Not only is anything to do with coconuts great for weight loss, but it is a great sexual aid, as it also helps the body's circulation. It has been known to aid male sexuality and coconut milk and honey is an excellent concoction to stimulate sexual desire (in fact among Malaysians, it is known to be a cure in the bedroom). Coconut water has all the necessary minerals, vitamins, including great sugars and carbohydrates; it is a balanced electrolyte supplement rich in calcium, potassium, and magnesium.

Salt: For condiments, sea, or rock salt is recommended as regular salt will contract you and is way too yang for the human body creating blocked energy, as opposed to light expansive energy. Salt has a way of decreasing adrenal function and makes your kidneys tight. The more adrenal fatigue you will have, the greater will be your craving for salt, and the more fluid you are likely to hold on to. Aldosterone is a hormone that is produced in the adrenal cortex, responsible for the sodium, potassium, magnesium, and chloride levels in the blood, intestinal lining, and individual cells, influencing fluid and volume. The molecular structure of this sodium-potassium balance is the same as sea water, with different concentrations in the cells and in the intestinal lining. You may have heard the doctor tell you or any one of your family members at some point that your electrolytes are out of balance, especially when one is sick, and asked you to drink a lot of electral. This basically means that these minerals are out of the ratios required in your body. In adrenal fatigue, you crave salt because it is a direct result of the lack of requisite aldosterone. Low aldosterone levels impact sodium and potassium levels—a deficient diet or dieting in general and stress can lead to this. When sodium levels drop, water gets pulled out of your body, reducing sodium levels further, and you crave salt. One of the best ways to replenish the body's sodium-potassium levels is drinking small and frequent doses of water accompanied by some sea salt sprinkled over food or a concoction made of sea salt and sesame seeds called Gomashio (ratio 1:18) which will aid sexual vitality. The combination of both sea salt and sesame seeds in the ratio recommended provides a balance of minerals to natural oils boosting the circulatory system, which provides a resilience to body tissues and skin. On the other hand, an excess of regular table salt will make you hold on to water and store it under the layers of your skin, giving you that bloated feeling and increasing adrenal fatigue.

Tiny seeds of love: Sesame seeds have the highest source of selenium, plenty of zinc, calcium, iron, magnesium, vitamin E, folic acid, omega-3, omega-6, and EFAs. Once ground (as suggested above on how to make gomashio), it releases their minerals. Gomashio must be included daily in your diet. Make it and put in a shaker on your dining table.

Aphrodisiacs: The word comes from the name of the Greek goddess of sexuality and love—Aphrodite. Aphrodisiacs stimulate sexual desire through nutrition rather than casting some magic spell on you. In the ayurvedic text, the Caraka Samhita Vol III, three whole chapters have been dedicated to the study of 'Vajikarna therapy' i.e. how aphrodisiacs work. They have been classified in the foods that help in the prevention of diseases and rejuvenation and maintainance of positive health.

Spices: Spices stimulate sexual arousal but must be used in moderation as too much of it will cause a very yin effect, dispersing sexual energy. For eg. chillies have capsaicin which is known to stimulate sexual desire as it improves blood circulation.

Ginger: Ginger is known to stimulate erectile function and prolongs it. It is an aphrodisiac and also thins blood; it has trace mineral iron, zinc, and magnesium. It contains vitamin C, beta carotene, calcium, iron, and magnesium.

Garlic: Garlic increases circulation and keeps the blood vessels clean. It is also high on calcium. It's rich in calcium and vitamin C.

Saffron (Kesar): Saffron is known to be sexually stimulating; a particular Asian variety increases male libido. Men have used it to prevent premature ejaculation. It improves blood circulation and helps the kidneys. A pinch before bedtime will also aid in overcoming sleeping disorders.

Nutmeg (Jayphal): It is known to stimulate nerve cells and aid blood circulation.

Basil (Tulsi): Also called holy basil by Hindus and now hailed in the West, basil is regarded as an 'anti-stress' agent. It is known to purify blood and help with respiratory disorders. Basil stimulates sex drive and boost fertility.

Turmeric: Turmeric has antioxidants, is known to be an anti-bacterial agent, and also 'revs up' sex drive.

High quality unrefined vegetable oils are good to prepare food in, not the extra refined variety. Coffee, tea, alcohol, drugs, medication should be minimized. Herbal teas and decaffeinated teas are recommended.

Additional antioxidant super foods include:

Chia seeds: (known as takmarya or subja) for their excellent source of omega 3 and phytonutrients. They are also highly antioxidant (kaempferol, chlorogenic acid, caffeic acid, and querecetin) in nature. It contains a host of trace minerals which are lacking in the Indian diet. It also contains all the necessary amino acids, making it a seed which is high on protein.

Goji berries: Goji berries are native to Tibet and China and are very high on amino acid profile, therefore considered the most nutritious among all fruits. They impact your sexual drive positively as they are high on arginine, affecting the production of NO. They are also high on antioxidants like selenium and beta carotene and prevent damage by free radicals. Recommended daily allowance is 10–30 gms. A word of caution—do not take them if you are on blood thinners.

MACA: MACA is a Peruvian plant (not available in India) which is used for strength and fertility in traditional medicine. Also considered to be an aphrodisiac amongst the Incas. It has a particular chemical called p-methoxybenzyl isothiocyanate which is known to enhance sexual drive. It is known to reduce enlarged prostate glands and improve erectile function. It has phytochemicals in large numbers and is known to also control high estrogen levels.

> 'All you need is love. But a little chocolate now and then doesn't hurt'
>
> CHARLES M. SCHULZ.

Apart from sinful bonding after love with your mate, a little dark decadence of chocolate goes a long way. It is the most popular food when it comes to sexuality. The Aztecs referred to it as 'nourishment of the Gods'. Did you know the emperor Montezuma consumed 50 glasses of home-sweetened chocolate to maintain his virility and potency before visiting his harem of more than 600 women? Chocolate is also referred to as *kryptonite*—nutritional gold. Chocolate provides a wide array of benefits—a powerful antioxidant and rich in minerals like potassium, copper, magnesium and iron—it is known to stimulate endorphins, so will put you in a positive state of mind, enhancing pleasure as it contains serotonin (anti-depressant). Flavonoids in cocoa protect your heart, and keeps blood flowing to the heart. It is also known to prevent formation of LDL cholesterol in your blood vessels—chocolate is a major source of nitric oxide. It keeps your blood pressure under control and scores over red wine, green tea in phenols and flavonoids. It also contains phenylethyamine (PEA, also called the love drug), a compound (trace amino acid) which makes dopamine affecting arousal and enhancing mood. When buying chocolate dark chocolate, it is best to buy one without sugar. A word of caution—all the varieties available in the Indian market claiming no sugar have a derivative of sugar. So when I'm advocating dark, I mean 85 percent should be pure dark chocolate with no sugar additives.

Boosting Yang

Men should definitely have higher yang and people who are yang depleted can boost it by increasing the Essential Fatty Acids (peanuts, avocados—have B6 and B3 vital for sexual performance, fish and flax seed oil) in their diet to boost testosterone levels, boost protein levels, and keeping the simple sugars out by using herbs like Siberian ginseng or shilajit. Include foods like garlic, oysters, radish, turnips, mushrooms, onions, leeks, whole grains, red pumpkin, ginger, mustard greens (sarson), cherries, apples, bananas, quinoa, kidney beans, lentil, black beans, walnuts, cruciferous vegetables—broccoli, cauliflower and cabbage, and avoid caffeine, moderate alcohol, avoid excess salt, and use chromium supplements to boost metabolism by enhancing the action of insulin and zinc.

Yang boosting Love Tea

(makes blend for 15 cups and can be stored in the fridge)

Ingredients

- 1 tbs garam masala
- 1 tbs cardamom
- ½ cup regular tea leaves

Method

To make 1 cup of tea, use 2 teaspoons of this mixture. Add to boiling water. Cover the concoction and keep for 10 minutes before serving. Add ginger slices when steeping.

Boosting yin

Women and men who are yin depleted must cut back on animal foods and nourish yin with beetroot, spinach, cucumber, grapes, berries, watermelon, red pumpkin, eggplant, millets, amaranth, tofu, mung beans, seeds, apples, beans, papaya, pomegranates, tomatoes, sweet potatoes, barley, sprouts, flaxseeds, chickpeas, and garlic. They need a lot of potassium as the body makes estrogen with it. Good sources of potassium are whole grains, legumes, fresh fruits, and vegetables. They must drink a lot of water, avoid caffeine and alcohol, and go off medication unless they are prescribed medication for some specific health condition. Medications depletes yin. Take good

EFAs (mentioned in yang boosting foods) and take a calcium magnesium supplement.

Yin boosting love tea

MAKES 1 CUP

Ingredients

   1 tsp crushed ginger
   Pinch of cinnamon
   ½ tsp honey
   10 – 12 strands of saffron

Method

Bring water to a boil in a pan (a little over 1 cup). Add ginger, honey, and cinnamon to the water when it first boils. Turn down the heat and add the saffron strands. Cover and let it simmer for approximately 15 minutes. Turn the flame off and let it steep for an additional 5 minutes. Strain and serve warm.

Foods that will help you sleep

Trace minerals are known to aid the body's electrical activity in the nervous system, which impacts your sleep. Lack of these will cause depression, blood sugar issues, PMS, a nervous and stressed condition, faster ageing, and a loss of memory. So here is a list of trace minerals and their sources:

Chromium

Chromium mainly manages your blood sugar as it aids the release of insulin. Imbalance of chromium will hinder sleep and will play havoc with blood sugars needed for normal sleep activity. The body needs sustained sugars to maintain brain activity as the brain's main source of energy is glucose (chromium is the active component of Glucose Tolerant Factor [GTF]). The primary function of GTF is to increase the action of insulin. Insulin is responsible for carrying sugar (glucose) to the cells. Waking up at night is a sign of a drop in blood sugar levels and an increase in adrenaline levels. Good sources of chromium include fish, poultry products (eggs [has zinc, magnesium, B vitamins, and protein] and chicken), whole grains, potatoes, and fruit.

Chlorophyll

Chlorophyll makes blood in plants and will make good blood in you. It will build oxygen which carries red blood cells, will promote good adrenal activity impacting energy, will detoxify the liver, and is anti-inflammatory. Chlorophyll is found in leafy greens and spirulina.

Calcium

In conjunction with magnesium, calcium helps regulate heart beat and monitor the blood pressure. It aids communication between nerves—the ones that also help with the relaxation response, especially neurotransmitters. Calcium is found in green leafy vegetables, fish, sunflower seeds, kidney beans, apples, barley, buckwheat (kuttu), beetroot, pumpkin, nuts, turkey, coconuts, eggs, and dairy.

Copper

Copper ensures that oxygen is delivered to the brain while you sleep. It manages blood sugar and controls high blood pressure that can interfere with the stages of sleep. It is found in lentils, bananas, any white beans (chowli, white kidney beans), dark green vegetables, nuts, sesame seeds, pumpkin seeds, dried herbs, liver, and fish.

Iron

Iron ensures that your blood condition is good as it is responsible for haemoglobin—the primary function of haemoglobin is to carry oxygen to the brain during sleep. Iron is found in whole grains, beetroots, raisins, apricots, leafy greens, chicken, nuts, legumes, dark chocolate, and tofu.

Magnesium

A co-factor for the absorption of calcium-magnesium is absolutely essential in your diet. While calcium supports contraction in the body, magnesium supports relaxation. Also called the 'relaxation mineral', without magnesium your muscles and your heart will be weak, causing anxiety, insomnia, and tension. Magnesium is found in all leafy green vegetables, figs, sweet potatoes, bananas, apricots, tuna, beetroot, dark chocolate, pumpkin seeds, flax and sesame seeds, almonds, pine nuts (chilgoza), cashews, coconuts, and soybean.

Iodine

Iodine is essential for thyroid health (in the case of an under-active thyroid), without which you will lack energy and it will impact sleep and libido. Iodine is found in spirulina, beans, turnips (shalgam), cucumber, okra (bhindi), leafy greens, straw-berries, watermelon, and sea salt (iodized).

Potassium

The potassium-sodium balance (electrolyte balance) is crucial for proper cardiovascular health. Not only does potassium increase stamina, it also makes your muscles function better. If you are taking drugs or are drinking excessive coffee and alcohol, then you are susceptible to it being leached out of your system.

Food sources include bananas, yellow melons, avocados, leafy greens, coconuts, and fish.

Other than these trace minerals, you must get a healthy dose of all your **Essential Fatty Acids (EFAs)**, the omega 3 and omega 6, only obtained through food sources as the body does not make these. They are also responsible for testosterone production as mentioned earlier, and also smooth nerve functioning, normalizing sleep and supplying you with the right neurotransmitters. Food sources are chia and flax seeds, tuna, sardines, mackerel, salmon, pinenuts, almonds, sesame/sunflower/pumpkin seeds, all whole grains, and dark and leafy greens.

Another big sleep aid is **Vitamin C.** It converts tryptophan to serotonin which governs sleep patterns. It is found in all berries, kiwi, apples, mangoes (rich in beta carotene, required for sex hormones estrogen and testosterone, Vitamin C), papayas, pineapples, papaya, all citrus fruit, potatoes, figs, greens like broccoli, peppers, leafy greens, mung and alfalfa sprouts, beetroot, sweet potatoes, and red and green chillies.

Vitamins **B3, B5, and B6**: B3 balances blood sugar, B5 protects the adrenals from the onslaught of stress, and B6 uplifts your mood also aids tryptophan convert to serotonin. Sources are whole grains, of which brown rice is king, legumes, avocados, asparagus, mushrooms, bok choy, broccoli, potatoes, chicken, eggs, fish, sunflower seeds, avocados (also rich in potassium), and nuts.

Avoid foods that have tyramine derived from an amino acid called tyrosine, which increases norepinephrine which will hamper sleep and also trigger headaches. Foods which are aged i.e. fermented like cheese, some types of beer, smoked fish, sugar, chocolate, eggplant, tomatoes, and potatoes. While I recommend sauerkraut, it shouldn't be eaten right before bedtime.

Lovers snacks

1. *Popcorn:* Very rich in amino acids and L-arginine where Nitric Oxide is generated. Makes for an excellent lovers snack.

2. *Celery sticks:* Boost your sex hormones. The root of celery is actually considered to be an aphrodisiac, and it contains beta-carotene, folic acid, and B6. Excellent digestive also—good after a heavy meal and before making love.

3. *Figs:* Symbolize sexuality; their high beta-carotene fuels the sex hormones, increases libido, and reduces stress. Contains vitamin C and calcium.

4. *Mood food:* A banana contains bufotenine, an alkaloid which elevates your mood and sex drive. Vitamin B6 will give you that good serotonin. So if you are feeling blue, eat a banana before you meet your mate for a date.

For maximum energy: Focus on nutrient dense foods which will reduce the stress response and allow the body to conserve energy, to be used as fuel. The nutrient dense foods have been enumerated in all the food elements laid out for you earlier in this chapter. The guidelines that you should follow for gaining maximum energy are: drink 1 nutritious smoothie a day, try eating 1 salad daily (cooked or raw)—raw will give you more enzymes, but if you have a weak stomach, I recommend short cooked like using sautéed vegetables, or steamed in a salad—eat throughout the day, and eat a substantial afternoon/evening snack: preferably something high on protein or a superfood.

Part 2

The LOVE Diet

The 3 diets for love

I have tried to introduce diets that would work across the board for all types of food lovers. The 'International Love Diet' is a plan for people who love to try different cuisines and is a plan for vegetarians and non-vegetarians. The 'Indian Love Diet' is for those of you, who enjoy eating Indian cuisine and is again for non-vegetarians and vegetarians. The 'All-Embracing Love Diet' is a simpler diet than the first two, and is only vegetarian.

Since the 'International Love Diet' and the 'Indian Love Diet' have non-vegetarian dishes, you can look up the vegetarian portions of these diets in the 'sattvik' diet—all-cuisine or an Indian cuisine approach to cooking. These portions are sattvik in nature.

> *Sattvik* food produces a calmer mind and emotions. Sattvik food is charged with prana or life force, and it necessarily implies vegetarian food. Food prepared with 'love' will add to the sattvik quality of the food.

ALL CUISINES LOVE DIET

	MONDAY	TUESDAY	WEDNESDAY	THURSDAY	FRIDAY	SATURDAY	SUNDAY
BREAKFAST	Strawberry Kissed Banana Smoothie	Banana Bliss & Pineapple Smoothie	Love Grapes & Greens Juice	Blushing Papaya & Banana Smoothie	Gorgeous Greens Smoothie	Tantalizing Mixed Fruit & Berry Smoothie	Antioxidant Pomegranete Stress buster
SNACK	Fresh Fruit	Fresh Fruit	Fresh Fruit	Fresh Fruit	Fresh Fruit	Fresh Fruit	Fresh Fruit
LUNCH	Veg: Quintessential Quesadillas and Greens Salad	Veg: Scrumptious whole wheat Spaghetti with olives & lemon	Veg: Merry Moroccan Veggies with quinoa	Veg: Rapturesque Refried Beans Corn Tortillas Bell Peppers Marinated	Veg: Craving Chick-pea like Salad & Luscious Stamina Stuffed Qunioa Bell Peppers	Veg: Flavoured Fusilli Salad & Spicy Sensual Tomato Soup	Veg: Tantalizing Tofu & Broccoli in Sweet & Sour Sauce Brown Rice

	MONDAY	TUESDAY	WEDNESDAY	THURSDAY	FRIDAY	SATURDAY	SUNDAY
	Non Veg:	Non Veg:	Non Veg:	Non Veg:	Non Veg:	Non Veg:	Non Veg:
	Surreal Shrimp Chilli and Basil with Quinoa Pilaf	Tenacious Tuna & Tomato Salad Whole Wheat Toast	Gratifying Goa prawn curry with brown rice	Wholesome Whole Wheat Buns Fish Burgers Fillers: Greens Tomato/ Cucumber	Pep-me-up Pasta Salad with shrimp, roasted peppers	Succulent Steamed Basa with Quinoa Pilaf Side: Vegetables Boiled/ Steamed	Flamboyant Fish & Noodle Soup with Waldorf Salad
EVENING SNACK							
	Crispbread with Nut Butter like Peanut/ Almond	Sensual Superfood Trail Mix	Attraction Building Almond, Fig, & Cacao Bars	Gluten Free Chocolate Cake Slice	Heavenly Poached Pears	Almond Milk 1 glass Watermelon Salad	Lustful Raw Chocolate Bars
	Yin/Yang Love Tea	Yin/Yang Love Tea	Yin/Yang Love Tea	Yin/Yang Love Tea	Yin/Yang Love Tea	Yin/Yang Love Tea	Yin/Yang Love Tea

DINNER

	MONDAY	TUESDAY	WEDNESDAY	THURSDAY	FRIDAY	SATURDAY	SUNDAY
Veg:	*Miso Soup Mouthwatering Mint Coucous with Vegetables	*Pumpkin Soup Bashful Baked Mushrooms Tomato (Garlic)	*Cauliflower Red P Soup Scintillating Stir Fried Veggies Exotic Lentils Brown Rice	*Lentil soup Luring Quinoa Tabouleh with Greens Salad	*Carrot Dahl Soup Energized Chickpeas Bak Choy with Brown Rice	Stir fry tofu and black bean Green Salad	*Tomato Soup Creamy Barley Rissoto Roasted Pumpkin
Non Veg:	Spunky Sweet & Sour Fish Steamed Veggies	Flavourful Soba with Fish & Vegetables	Juicy Baked Fish ginger dressing served with noodles	Asian Salmon with Brown Rice	Passionate Pan Fried Fish with Ras el hanout Brown Rice	Aphrodisi-ac-al Seafood & Eggplant Salad	Sizzling Thai style Fish with Minted Couscous

*Soup remains common to non-vegetarians

Monday	Tuesday	Wednesday	Thursday	Friday	Saturday	Sunday
AFTER DINNER SNACK						
Lovers Soy Yogurt with Strawberries	Merry Melon Fruit Salad	Juicy Pomegranete with Lime	Romantic Banana & Strawbery Non-dairy Ice Cream	Ambrosia Pear & Fig Compote	Baked/ Poached Pear with raisins	Wild Berry Compote

INDIAN LOVE DIET

	MONDAY	TUESDAY	WEDNESDAY	THURSDAY	FRIDAY	SATURDAY	SUNDAY
BREAKFAST	Wholesome Rice Cream Porridge	Indian Chinch Bhaat	Sustained Sugars Foxtail Millet Poha	Brown Rice Idlis Coconut Chutney	Brown Rice Poha	Fresh Fruit Platter	Brown Rice Dosas
SNACK	Seasonal Fresh Fruit	Seasonal Fresh Fruit	Seasonal Fresh Fruit	Seasonal Fresh Fruit	Seasonal Fresh Fruit	Foxtail Millet Poha	Seasonal Fresh Fruit
LUNCH	Veg: Brown Rice with Yellow Lentils with Green Peppers Mushrooms	Veg: Millet (Fox Tail) Green Mung Salad Cabbage Green Sauce	Veg: Amaranth & Jovar rotis with Chickpeas Split Green Lentils Salad	Veg: Quinoa Pilaf Red Kidney Bean Curry Sweet Potatoes with Cumin	Veg: Brown Rice Brown Lentils ginger Garlic Spinach	Veg: Wheat Couscous White Beans Borolloti VEGAN	Veg: Brown Rice Curried Lentils Mixed Peppers

	MONDAY	TUESDAY	WEDNESDAY	THURSDAY	FRIDAY	SATURDAY	SUNDAY
EVENING SNACK	Peace-loving Mung Dahl Chillas Yin/Yang Love Tea	Steamed Muthias Yin/Yang Love Tea	Seratonin-rich Sweet Potato Lime and Corriander Yin/Yang Love Tea	Natural Sugar booster Red Pumpkin with basil/garlic Yin/Yang Love Tea	Tempered Idlis Yin/Yang Love Tea	Corn sauteed in lime and chilli Yin/Yang Love Tea	Sweet Potato Pancakes Yin/Yang Love Tea
DINNER	Non Veg: Fish Masala Pan Fried Garlic Spinach Amaranth & Jovar Rotis	Non Veg: Fish Curry in Coconut Milk with Brown Rice & Fenugreek Leaves (Methi)	Non Veg: Lemon & Olive Oil Steamed Fish Quinoa Pilaf add Veggie made in Basil Pesto	Non Veg: Goan Shrimp Curry with Brown Rice Amaranth Leaves (cholai)	Non Veg: Shrimp Chilli Basil with Mushy Brown Rice	Non Veg: Kerela Fish Curry brown rice Green Beans	Non Veg: Potato & Tuna Salad

MONDAY	TUESDAY	WEDNESDAY	THURSDAY	FRIDAY	SATURDAY	SUNDAY
			EVENING SNACK			
Lovers Soy Yogurt with Strawberries	Merry Melon Fruit Salad	Juicy Pomegranete with Lime	Romantic Banana & Strawberry Ice Non-dairy Ice Cream	Ambrosia Pear & Fig Compote	Baked/ Poached Pear with raisins	Wild Berry Compote

**Substitute Lunch for dinner & dinner for lunch in case you want a non-veg lunch or vice versa

SATVIK DIET

	MONDAY	TUESDAY	WEDNESDAY	THURSDAY	FRIDAY	SATURDAY	SUNDAY
BREAKFAST	Strawberry Banana Smoothie	Banana Bliss & Berry Smoothie	Love Grape & Celery Juice	Compassionate Papaya & Banana Smoothie	Gorgeous Greens Smoothie	Mixed Fruit & Berry Smoothie	Antioxidant Pomegranate Booster
SNACK	Passionate Fruit Jello	Seasonal Fresh Fruit	Joyful Fruit Salad	Seasonal Fresh Fruit	Orange Agar Gel	Sweet Nectar Ambrosia	Grape Pineapple Jello
LUNCH	Veg: Karma Casserole	Veg: Aura Cleanse Asian Stir Fry with Brown Rice	Veg: Whole Wheat Spaghetti and Pure Meat-less Meat Balls	Veg: Calming Yellow Lentils Mushroom & Green Peppers with Brown Rice (yours)	Veg: Divine Burrito - with Black beans	Veg: Energetic Quinoa Stuffed in Bell Peppers	Veg: Wild Mushroom Quinoa Pilaf with yellow lentils

	MONDAY	TUESDAY	WEDNESDAY	THURSDAY	FRIDAY	SATURDAY	SUNDAY
EVENING SNACK	Fig Apple Compote	Curried Fruit	Poached Pears	Happy Baked Curried Bananas	Green Earth Dip with Veggie Sticks	Robust Roasted Spiced Mix Nuts	Heavenly Coconut Ice Cream
	Yin/Yang Love Tea	Yin/Yang Love Tea	Yin/Yang Love Tea	Yin/Yang Love Tea	Yin/Yang Love Tea	Yin/Yang Love Tea	Yin/Yang Love Tea
DINNER	*Miso Soup Garlic Spinach Brown Rice Yellow Lentils with Bottle Gourd	*Pumpkin Soup Cauliflower & Corriander Mash Amaranth and Sorghum Chapatis	*Cauliflower Red P Soup Soba Noodles or Whole Wheat and Pea Pesto	*Lentil soup Curried Greens Quinoa Pilaf Green Mung Lentils	*Carrot Lentil Soup Tomato Curry Mildly Spiced Fenugreek Leaves Brown Rice	Roasted Squash Soup Vegetable Stew Quinoa with Peas or Sorghum Rotis	*Tomato Soup Vegetable Kebabs Amaranth Sorghum Rotis Yellow Mung Dahl

	Monday	Tuesday	Wednesday	Thursday	Friday	Saturday	Sunday
			AFTER DINNER SNACK				
	Spiced Hot Almond Milk Or Ginger Tea	Golden Milk (Cashew and Almonds) Or Ginger Tea	Naturally Sweet Almond Date Milk Or Ginger Tea	Energy Building Rice Ginger Milk Or Ginger Tea	Spiced Hot Almond Milk Or Ginger Tea	Hot Date Milk Or Ginger Tea	Energy Building Rice Ginger Milk Or Ginger Tea

** All milk is non-dairy milk

Sexuality and ageing

> 'I don't think about ageing. I have those moments
> of panic and vanity. But life keeps getting better, so
> you can't worry about it too much.'
>
> JENNIFER GARNER

Sexual behaviour and desire change with ageing, but they never really go away. Sometimes health issues impact sexuality, but the need for intimacy—both emotional and physical—remains even as you become older and more settled. The key to be in touch with your sexuality when you age is to keep talking to your partner. Talk, take your health seriously, and listen. For women, it's usually their gynaecologist and for men, it's usually their women. If you don't have a partner then talk to a friend. It is extremely important to build a relationship at this time with your healthcare provider—this could be your doctor or for men, a urologist.

For women, menopause may lead to a waning of sexual desire or sometimes not—it's just a matter of adapting to changes. At this time it is good address your and your partner's sexual needs. Does a low libido alter or change anything about your life? I recently spoke to a cousin who is 46. She said that perimenopause phase is really nerve wracking, not only emotionally, but physically as well. The same was revealed to me by a friend yesterday—she's 50 and going through menopause. The sheer physicality of the situation has taken a toll on her nerves. But when I asked them if it has affected things between them and their partners, they surprisingly said that nothing much had changed about their sexuality or sexual behaviour. They both have very supportive partners and it really helped. It's important for men to extend a hand of support to their lady loves.

Your sexual health and fitness are affected dramatically if you suffer from vaginal dryness. In such a case, first get it examined by your gynaecologist. Once the diagnosis is confirmed, then treatment could range from using lubricants during sex, to more frequent sex, avoiding douching, extending foreplay time with your partner, and the hip bath recommended on page 186.

For men, not only is testosterone affected with age, keeping their prostate gland examined is crucial. Prostatitis is an inflammation of the prostate gland, which happens with age. Eighty percent of men suffer from this; it may or may not interfere with their lifestyle. However, a good thing to do is go for a physical examination and get your PSA (prostate specific antigen) test done regularly—especially after the age of 40. Usually men under 35 suffer from acute bacterial prostatitis (ABP). Its symptoms include frequent urination, chills and fever, pain in joints, muscles and lower back, pain in ejaculation, pain during urination, inability to empty bladder completely, and feeling like you need to urinate, sometimes accompanied with pain. Those who work out or engage in sport are prone to an *inguinal hernia*—when a part of the intestine protrudes from a weak spot in muscle or connective tissue holding the organ in place. Most times it occurs like a bulge, and you can push it back in, but at times you can't and that's when you need medical intervention. Women are also prone to them. The treatment is usually surgery for this type of hernia. It's important to seek treatment as it can compromise your sexual health by causing pain during sex, and will curtail sexual activity and pleasure.

ADRENAL FATIGUE

If you suffer from adrenal fatigue, you will do best by combining fat, protein, and starchy carbohydrates (such as whole grains) at every meal and at every snack. When eaten together, they provide a steady source of energy over a longer period of time because they are converted into glucose at different rates. The starchy carbohydrates get converted pretty quickly, the protein takes longer, and the fats take the longest to convert into energy. Combining these three is the perfect answer for an adrenal energizing meal.

STRATEGIES TO ENHANCE SEXUALITY

1. Limit alcohol consumption
2. Avoid tobacco
3. Get off medications
4. Be at peak energy levels
5. Maintain your health
6. Share your thoughts, desires—COMMUNICATE
7. Build up sensual intimacy (massage, touching, non-verbal cues, cuddling)
8. Make time
9. Put all major issues like finances, and kids on the back burner when alone with your partner
10. Plan a getaway
11. Be spontaneous
12. Don't rush into sexual play
13. Keep away phone, iPads, iPods
14. Be mindful—be present—be in the NOW

Getting older is not a disease—you are in charge of your sexuality and the love life you want. While *ageing is a fact, feeling old is optional*. The best thing you can do is stay sexually active. I keep setting new fitness milestones for myself every year— my next one is to participate in the Wildflower Triathalon held in California—that's how I keep myself challenged. Overcome your fears by challenging yourself constantly and keeping yourself mentally and physically fit.

Remedies to revive sexual health

Vitality stew (for vegetarians, replace fish with burdock)

Objective: To restore sexual vitality, energy, and potency

Ingredients

    1 whole fish, including bones (about 2.5 kgs)
    ½ to 1 cup tulsi leaves with stem
    1 tbs grated ginger (fresh)

Burdock equal proportion to fish (dhatura ki jad in hindi or ghagra in Marathi); native mostly to Africa and Europe. Some Northern parts of India are growing this root vegetable). You can substitute with carrots instead, if burdock is not easily available.

Method

Leave fish intact, except cleaning it to remove internals (gall bladder and thyroid). Include the whole fish i.e. the head, scales, and fins; you can remove the eye of the fish if you wish. Cut it into 1 – 2 inches thick pieces.

Cut burdock root (ideal is 2 – 3 times the weight of the fish) into match sticks or thin slices. Chop everything else, and place all ingredients in a pressure cooker. Take tulsi leaves and stems and wrap it in a muslin cloth and tie the end like a pouch. Put this in the pressure cooker on top of the fish, and add water 3 – 4 cups (²/₃ʳᵈ water). Pressure cook for an hour on low flame. Once done switch off and let pressure release on its own, don't force it. Alternatively you can boil the soup for 6 hours till bones dissolve.

This soup can be kept in the fridge for up to 5 days.

Eat 1 cup at a time—warm. You can continue to have it till you vitality returning.

Hip bath and douche

Objective: Relieve sexual organ disorders in women, like fibroids, cysts, and vaginal infections

Method

To prepare the hip bath, run hot water in a bath tub. You can get a regular tub from the market that can take you sitting in the tub with hips immersed and legs outside. Dry radish leaves in the sun for 2-3 days, then boil in water (about 2 litres can be boiled and then some warm water can be added just so when you sit in the tub it covers your hips) and add several handfuls of sea salt. Use enough water to cover up to your hip area while you are sitting down in the tub. Wrap a towel around you while you are sitting in the water to encourage sweating. If the water cools down, then add more hot water to the tub. Sit in this water for at least 20 minutes.

The hot water will activate blood circulation in your lower body and your skin may turn red. This blood circulation will loosen fat deposits (that is why the white radish leaves also help) and mucous accumulated in this region.

Following the hip bath, make a douche of warm water, juice of half a lime, and a pinch of sea salt. The douche will further loosen fat and mucous that has been dislodged while you took the hip bath. You can repeat a hip bath three times a week for at least 6 weeks. Please make sure that your diet is clean, and not building fats and mucous again, which include foods like cheese, dairy, eggs, sugar, meats, all foods that contain saturated fats, and cholesterol.

Your love health

Movement and exercise have been a part of my life since I was very young. My father would tell me how I was thrown in the pool when I was 5-months-old by the nurses of the hospital I was born in. I was born in England, and apparently they do that to babies there as part of some kind of therapy. So naturally I took to the water, and swimming has been an essential part of my life. In school, I would play sports of all kinds—from hockey to long distance running, high jumps, long jumps, the works. In college, in the quest to stay thin, it was Jane Fonda, kick boxing, step aerobics, and many other such fads. However, the one thing that happened over the years is that movement and exercise have become a habit, like brushing your teeth ever morning. After many years of going at it, in my early 30s I realized you have to gravitate towards something that sustains you, and keep challenging yourself every year. For me it is swimming, Yogalates (I am a certified Yogalates [that's a combination of Yoga and Pilates] teacher from the Yoga Pilates Academy, Australia), and some light band work. Pick exercises which become part of your day-to-day life and are easy for the body to sustain.

Sexual health and fitness is maintained through a combination of exercise, sharpening the mind, with the bedrock of a solid diet. It is about having the continuous ability to enjoy sex the way you want, for as long as you want and with, the person(s) you are attracted to. A healthy body is a sexy body. You don't have to be a guy with a six pack, or a woman with an hourglass figure, but you need to be fit—that is, have stamina and endurance. Small changes in your day-to-day life will take you a long way. Your accumulation of lifestyle habits is what defines you today and will also define you tomorrow. If you are a smoker, heavy meat eater, abuse alcohol—your body will show signs of ageing faster. You must have what is termed as 'dynamic fitness'—the ability of the body to move vigorously and with minimal effort. This is generally a combination of cardiovascular fitness, endurance, flexibility, balance, and speed. This type of fitness declines when you are post your mid 30s, which is why it's important to keep challenging yourself. To build up 'stamina' you need sustained training. Ask yourself questions like how do you feel at the end of your day? Do you still have the energy to go out for dinner with your partner or spend some time together?

Circulation is the key here and so is breathing. I have explained in an earlier chapter how circulation is affected by your diet, impacting your blood vessels and heart. Good circulation makes you receptive to sexual arousal and love. Interrupting the body's ability to let blood flow freely is like putting a roadblock in your love life. Your skin, ovaries, and haemoglobin are all dependent on oxygen. So, deep breathing and pranayams are always helpful and a good incorporation in your daily life.

Smokers have almost next to nothing oxygenating their cells. Carbon monoxide uses up all the available haemoglobin and the body makes extra haemoglobin to carry the oxygen they need, so they suffer from a misleading high haemoglobin. Smokers are taking oxygen away from their body and this in turn impacts sexual health. Exercise will not only bring in oxygen and increased circulation, but will also put you in a good mood with all those endorphins I mentioned to you.

Physical appearance is important to fuel your bedroom passions. Body posture says a lot about you—it gives away your age, confidence level, and also your state of health. How comfortable you are in your own skin will show the very first time you walk into a room of strangers. You need to pay attention to muscle tone and strengthening your core (stomach muscles) as they will make you stand up straighter, correct your slouch, and tighten your belly. Your leg muscles (thighs and butt) will also hold you together and make you move gracefully through the room and to your mate. When you make contact or shake hands, your hand muscles, arms, shoulders convey warmth and a connection. You must make sure that these are worked upon in your exercise regimen. Your body is the structure that you represent to the world and also the physical evidence of your 'sexuality', so make sure you spend some time on it. Remember a strong body equals a sexy body.

I have my own take on what makes for great love health as far as exercise is concerned. I am sure all of us include some amount of exercise in our daily lives, so please continue with whatever you do for cardio activity and strength training. However the areas that need a focus are:

1. **The core:** Strong abdominal and pelvic muscles and relaxed hips especially in women. Healthy PC muscles (puboccygeus) are very important. This will improve blood flow to the sexual areas, bring in bladder control, and enhance the love experience.

2. **Blood flow to hips:** Increased circulation and blood flow in your pelvic region will help with stamina, endurance, and will also sharpen your sexual sensitivity.

3. **Breathing:** Breathing exercises will help oxygen flow within the body, stimulate metabolism, aid digestion, and also release tension.

4. **Connecting the mind and body:** Lifting tension, focussing on positive thoughts, and meditating are key in tying it all together.

The core

1. **Engaging the core:** The muscles that shape the waist and keep your pelvic floor in great shape are called the transverse abdominis muscles (TA). Engaging these muscles is the key to strengthening your core. Place your first two fingers on the upper bone of your hips and if you cough, you will feel the TA muscle dance a bit under your fingers.

   As explained in the Kegels below, breathe in and balloon the belly out, then while you breathe out draw the navel to the spine. If you visualize that someone has put a 2 kilo rice bag on your belly, you'll get the picture. By drawing the belly in, you are engaging the TA. Repeat 10 times. (Advantages: Brings in sexual sensitivity to this area. Impacts chakras 1,2)

2. **Kegels:** This is the most well-known exercise developed by Dr Arnold Kegel in the 1940s intended to help women recover from incontinence due to childbirth. But it's the best thing to tone your pelvic floor muscles. Recent research with men using the Kegel exercise has shown that it is equally valuable to both genders. The pubococcygeus (PC) muscles are the ones that get engaged when you stop yourself from urinating—when you want to go but can't.

   So breathe in and let the belly balloon out (this is reverse breathing—also known as pilates breathing). Breathe out by pulling the navel down towards the spine (pretend someone has put a 2 kilo bag of rice on your navel). Breathe out and clench the muscles that stop you from urinating. Now there is a difference between engaging these muscles and your anus sphincter muscles, so be aware of that difference. Since you can stop yourself from urinating anytime, anywhere, these exercises can be done anytime, anywhere. It's called the 'invisible' core workout. Repeat this exercise 10 times. Kegels will also help delay the orgasm for you, besides also adding to the fact that you will achieve it, help with women who have lost their pelvic floor post childbirth, prevent urinary incontinence, and make you have super strong control of yourself. It prevents premature ejaculation in men, help them become multi-orgasmic (i.e. help them to have an orgasm without ejaculating), cure erectile dysfunction, help with prostate pain and swelling, and help bonding with your mate. This exercise impacts chakra 1 and 2.

3. **Ab switches:** Lie on your back. Bend you right knee towards your chest and interlace your fingers on the top of your shin. Next lift your left leg off the ground, pointing your toes, and lift your back off the floor. Touch your forehead to your knee, squeeze tightly through the core, and hold 4 breaths, repeat on other side. This exercise will give you a yummy tummy and a great butt. It impacts chakras 1, 2, 3, and 6.

Your hips

1. **The jelly fish:** Lie flat on your back. Bend your knees and lift them towards your chest, now fan them out, knees apart and toes touching. Start moving them in circles first clockwise then anti-clockwise 10 times in each rotation. This exercise transports blood to the pelvic region, strengthens hips and thighs, and builds flexibility and

mobility in the hip and pelvic region. It impacts chakras 1, 2, and 3.

2. **The clam:** Lie on your side with knees and legs bent in a 45 degree angle stacked on top of each other. Make sure your head is resting on your side arm (if required cushion it with a folded hand towel). Now spread-out your knees keeping toes together and bring them back. The burn is felt in your gluteus and buttock region. This exercise tones and strengthens muscles of the buttocks, firms inner and outer thighs, and stabilizes pelvis and hip rotators. It impacts chakras 1, 2, and 3.

3. **Pigeon:** Sit and take one leg back, while folding the other leg at the knee in front of you. Make sure the heel of the folded leg is in line with the knee of the stretched leg. Face forward. So now technically you are sitting on one buttock which is slightly lifted off the ground. Exhale bending forward at the waist, and lower your torso onto your right thighs (that is the bent knee leg). You will feel a stretch in the buttock of the bended knee. Breathe in and out here several times. This exercise stretches the groin, thighs, buttocks, and brings blood into this region. It impacts chakras 1 and 2.

Breathing

1. **Lumbar-thoracic breathe:** This is an excellent breathe to fill up your rib cage with that much-needed oxygen.

    Breathe 1: Now that we have a grip on the reverse breathing, lie flat on your back. Bend knees and feet at an angle (called supine rest position) breathe in, the belly balloons out and breathing out belly is drawn in, repeat this 10 times. This is belly breathe and also a great stress buster.

Breathe 2: The second phase is to breathe in (belly balloons out), breathe out, and pull the navel towards the spine and stop yourself from urinating (engaging the TA). Now keep this muscle engaged and breathe in. The breath will jump up into the rib cage, filling it up, and you may feel an expansion to the sides of the rib cage. This is Thoracic Lumbar breathe

I also recommend pranayama as expounded in the yoga tradition.

Connecting the mind and body

Meditation and love

Just as it's important to maintain your physical health, it is important to maintain good mental health. Your body will respond to how your mind is. Meditation is like plugging your energy switch everyday to the big power of the universe. It not only opens up all your energy pathways, but also makes your chakras vibrate at a higher frequency and opens you up in thoughts of love (we carve out new pathways for our thoughts to travel). Also if you have excess sexual energy, then meditation is a great way to channelize it in a healthy manner. Besides you can also choose to activate your heart chakra in a meditation sitting. No amount of meditation is beneficial, however, if your diet is not clean. I have practised Vipassana meditation for 18 years now, but initially when my diet was not great, I did not experience the benefits of meditation till I cleaned up my act. Increased endorphins released during meditation and help with sexual arousal when done in the long-term—I know I have felt this with my diet in place. DHEA secreted by the adrenal glands is secreted during meditation. DHEA circulates in the blood as DHEA-S (dehydroepiandrosterone-3 sulfate) which is a precursor for other hormones including estrogen and androgens.

Self love meditation for the heart chakra

Sit comfortably and relax with your hands in your lap. Imagine a small green (colour of the heart chakra) plant pushing up out of the ground, like a bulb in springtime. The shoot is being drawn upward by the warmth of the sun, and the more the sun shines, the taller the shoot grows. It sends itself outwards and the bulb opens and spread into leaves. The leaves are tilting themselves to catch the sun's rays, so that they can make food for this bud to grow further. The plant is a rich green, expanded and looking alive. At the peak of its growth, something new happens—a central bud forms that looks different. As you keep watching it, this central bud unfurls and becomes a pinkish red colour—a flower with delicate aroma and soft petals. Enjoy the colours and the contrast with the green and let this symbol relax and restore your heart chakra.

An attitude of gratitude

To me this is the single most powerful tool you can have to better your life, and take it onto another level when it comes to shifting to 'love'. Not only does having a genuine 'attitude of gratitude' signify that you are healthy in body, but also shows the health of your mind. As Louise Hay says, 'Gratitude is like a gear shift that can move our mental mechanism from obsession to peacefulness, from stuckness to creativity, from fear to love.'[1] By offering gratitude daily for all the things, people, situations in your life, you open up all your channels for things to come back to you from the universe in abundance. I feel, that over the years gratitude just becomes a practice, and when this happens you find that you can are grateful for even more things that

---

[1] Louise L. Hay. *You Can Heal Your Life*. Faber, 2008.

become a part of your life. Like my cousin and her husband offered me their home where I could finish this book—I can't thank them enough for doing this and every day after my morning meditation, I do my gratitude prayer and thank them. For many, a small situation will go unnoticed, but by being grateful for it, you actually enhance the power of your life to love back, and have tremendous compassion. For one, you stop feeling sorry for yourself. It raises your happiness quotient, takes you away from negatives in life, and infuses you with everything positive which brings in so much clarity.

Conclusion

I LOOK BACK AT THE RELATIONSHIPS our parents have had, yours and mine, and I think to myself—that was a good time. Our mums and dads accepted, tolerated, and loved their partners much more than we can ever hope to love our partners today. One of the reasons probably was that they didn't give themselves too many options and their food habits were simple. Unfortunately today's generation is different—we have choices, options, independence, which is all very great, but this leads to us being less tolerant and more demanding. This also stems out of how our food habits have deteriorated with the advent of modern fast food and junk food as we call it.

Are these changes for the better? Most of us have these romantic notions of love. I myself am a 'die hard' romantic. However, no relationship is perfect; there is no knight in shining armour waiting to rescue you or a perfect princess or harems (as most men would love to have). There are simple, loving individuals like you and me who are looking for love and just want someone to accept them for 'what they are' and not for 'what they are not'. Just accept the fact that compromises will have to be made, and there is no perfection. But there is great love in all of this, if you'd just care to look.

So this is me. I've gone through a fair bit of my life, lots of great loves came my way, and you may wonder, *why is she still single*? What I realize out of all these loves is there's nothing like first learning to love yourself so completely that compromise, compassionate love, giving, accepting—all become easy. The thing that shifted it for me has been food and a lifestyle full of things that give me back the 'love' from a larger consciousness —'the universe'. Do I sit here and crave the perfect relationship? The answer to that is 'no', but I believe that the love I come from is bound to bring in the love I give out, sooner or later. It already does in many fulfilling friendships and relationships I have. My food nourishes my spirit which is more important—I am connected to a larger purpose on this earth, not just my attachment to love for love's sake. Modern science sees food as carbohydrates, fats, and proteins. It does not understand the 'ki' or natural electromagnetic quality of food. The overriding question is: *Can modern civilization develop a food system to really nourish high quality vibration and consciousness in order to become peaceful and contribute to the larger world out of love?*

Our life is our dream on this earth. My dream was to bring Macrobiotics to India, and I think I have achieved this and am still in the process of spreading it further. But the precursor to all of this was changing my food. We can choose to formulate and create the life that we wish; it is entirely in our hands. As Michio Kushi says—can we strive to build 'One Peaceful World?'

Our life is eternal, though our human life is ephemeral. Our dream is endless, though our human desires are finite. The purpose of life—discovering, understanding, and becoming one with the infinite order of the universe—is imperishable. Like Shakespeare said, 'All the world's a stage, and all the men and women are merely players'. We live out our eternal dreams and relationships become our learning ground. We enjoy the freedom to change ourselves to adapt to the changing environment and to continue to develop endlessly. Happiness is the realization of our endless dream. After all, the question to ask yourself is—*Are we strengthening our environment with kindness, and are we full of love?*

Part 3

Recipes

HOT BEVERAGES

Almond milk

(Makes 1 cup)

Ingredients

  ½ cup almonds
  1 cup water

Method

1. Soak almonds for about 5 hours.
2. Grind with water and make milk; sieve and strain milk (using a cheesecloth/muslin cloth will help as one can squeeze the leftover almonds mash).
3. Leftover almonds can be used in your flour to make rotis.

Spiced hot almond milk

SERVES 2

Ingredients

  2 tsp honey or stevia

2 cups of almond milk

12 pistachios, shelled

6 cashews

6 almonds (blanched)

Pinch of saffron

Pinch of nutmeg (jaiphal)

2 tsp raisins

Method

Warm all the ingredients, mix in nuts and raisins.

Hot date milk

SERVES 2

Ingredients

2 tbs dates, pitted and chopped

1/4 tsp cinnamon

1 cup of almond milk

Method

Boil milk on low flame and add dates and cinnamon; simmer till dates become soft.

Golden milk

SERVES 3

Ingredients

2 tbs cashews

1 tbs raisins

3 tbs honey

3 cups almond milk

1 tsp turmeric

½ tsp nutmeg (jaiphal)

1/4 tsp saffron

Method

Mix all ingredients together and heat until warm. Add nuts and raisins once warm.

Rice milk

Make 2 cups

Ingredients

1 cup brown rice

5 cups water

Pinch of sea salt

Method

Boil the ingredients for 2 hours with a flame detector underneath the boiling pan—covered. Cook till water is half its original volume. Cool and sieve through a muslin cloth and squeeze out creamy liquid which is the rice cream. You can add some water to thin it down to be used as rice milk.

Energy building rice ginger milk

SERVES 2

Ingredients

2 cups rice milk

½ tsp ginger powder (sonth)

1 tbs honey

Method

Combine all the ingredients and warm.

SMOOTHIES

Strawberry kissed banana smoothie

SERVES 2

Ingredients

$^2/_3$ cup yogurt or soy yogurt

1½ cup coconut milk

1 tsp chia seeds

2 bananas

2 cups strawberries

Method

Blend all the above ingredients till creamy and serve chilled.

Banana bliss and pineapple smoothie

SERVES 1

Ingredients

1 cup cubed pineapple

1 medium banana, chopped

7 strawberries (optional)

1 cup soy yogurt

1 tsp vanilla extract (optional)

Some ice cubes

1 tsp flax seeds

Method

Blend all the above ingredients till creamy and serve with ice. Garnish with mint.

Love grapes and green juice

SERVES 2

Ingredients

    15 grapes (preferably red)
    4 celery sticks with leaves chopped (cut to 4 inches to put in juicer)

Method

Juice celery sticks first. Keep adding grapes and then greens. You can put the mix in a blender with ice just to get the crushed effect of ice.

Blushing papaya and banana smoothie

SERVES 2

Ingredients

    1 banana (cut into sizeable chunks)
    ½ papaya (cut into sizeable chunks)
    ½ cup soy yogurt
    1 tsp spirulina (optional)

Method

Blend all the above ingredients till creamy.

Gorgeous greens smoothie

SERVES 2

Ingredients

- 1 apple, chopped
- ½ cup water or vegetable stock
- 1 cup sprouts
- 1 tbs spirulina powder
- 2 tsp lemon juice
- 1 tsp wheat grass powder
- 4 tsb aloe vera juice
- ½ tsp cumin powder

Method

Put the fruit and water/stock in a blender, and blend until smooth. Add all other ingredients and blend again till it's consistent. Pour into glasses, mix in cumin powder, and enjoy!

Tantalizing mixed fruit and berry smoothie

SERVES 2

Ingredients

- ½ cup berries (any)
- 2 tbs pomegranate seeds
- 1 tbs sunflower or pumpkin seeds (unsalted)
- 1 tsp flax seeds
- 1 apple
- ½ papaya or 1 mango (if in season)
- ½ tsp of wheat grass powder
- ½ cup coconut milk

Method

Blend all the ingredients in a blender and pour over ice.

Antioxidant pomegranate stress buster

SERVES 2

Ingredients

  2 pomegranates
  2 oranges (optional)
  Some ice
  1 tsp chia seeds

Method

Put pomegranate seeds in a juicer. If using oranges then use a citrus juicer to extract juice from oranges. Blend together and pour over ice.

ENTRÉES

Karma casserole

SERVES 4

Ingredients

  2 tomatoes, sliced round
  ¾ cup tomato paste
  3 cups cooked whole wheat noodles
  1 cup cauliflower florets
  1 cup broccoli florets
  1 cup grated carrots
  ½ green bell pepper, minced
  ½ cup walnuts
  1 cup silken tofu, steamed and whipped in a bender
  Sea salt and black pepper to taste

Method

1. Steam all the vegetables, except the tomatoes.
2. Mix the tofu in the vegetables with noodles and tomato paste.
3. Pour this mix in a baking casserole.
4. Top with sliced tomatoes.
5. Bake at 175 degrees Celsius for 40 minutes.

Mouth watering mint couscous with vegetables

SERVES 4

Ingredients

1 carrot, cut into big chunks

1 turnip (shalgam), cut into quarters

1 zucchini, cut into 2 inch pieces (finger sizes)

½ sweet potato, cut into chunks

2 tomatoes, skin removed and chopped

2 tbs tomato paste (pureed in a blender)

1½ cups vegetable stock

1 tbs olive oil

2–3 garlic cloves, minced

1 tbs chilli powder

1 tsp cumin powder

½ tsp ginger, crushed

1 green chilly (optional)

1 bay leaf (tej patta)

Sea salt and black pepper to taste

Method

1. Pre-boil vegetables (you can pressure cook the turnips as they get done faster that way).

2. Warm oil in a wok. Add garlic and dry spices, and cook for 1–2 minutes. Add tomato paste and chopped tomatoes.

3. Add vegetable stock and bring to a boil.

4. Then add the vegetables and season with sea salt and pepper.

5. In a separate pan, make the couscous and add the mint. After it's done, cover with a cling wrap and keep covered till your vegetables get ready.

6. Open it up and fluff with a fork. Add the sea salt and pepper if required. Pour the vegetable mix over the couscous and serve warm.

Luring quinoa tabbouleh

SERVES 2

Ingredients

½ cup quinoa

2 green onions, side cut

1 tomato

½ cup boiled peas

A fistful of parsley

A fistful of coriander

2 tbs walnuts (optional)

Dressing

3 tbs extra virgin olive oil

1 tsp Dijon mustard

2 garlic pods, crushed

Juice of ½ lime

Sea salt and black pepper to taste

Method

1. Prepare quinoa by rinsing thoroughly and boiling in 1 cup of water.

2. When quinoa is done, add the chopped vegetables and coriander and parsley.

3. Mix together gently.

4. Mix in salad dressing.

5. Toast walnuts in a pan, chop roughly (after cooling), and toss into the tabbouleh.

Stir fry tofu and black beans

SERVES 2

Ingredients

½ cup black beans (rajma)

8 ounces of tofu, cubed

Small piece (½ inch) of ginger, sliced long

1–2 garlic cloves, minced

2 tbs corn, boiled

1 tsp toasted sesame oil

2 green onions, side cut

Sea salt and black pepper to taste

Method

1. Soak black beans overnight and pressure cook next day.

2. Heat oil in wok. Fry tofu on either side and set aside.

3. Add ginger and garlic to the same wok.

4. Add the black beans and corn and stir fry for 5 minutes on high flame.

5. Add tofu and cook for 2–3 minutes.

6. Season with sea salt and pepper.

7. Garnish with spring onions.

Spunky sweet and sour fish

SERVES 2

Ingredients

2 fillets of sea bass

½ onion, sliced thin

1 tomato, cut in quarters

3 spring onions, side cut

1 dry red chilly

1 tbs soy sauce

1 tbs fish sauce

3 garlic cloves, crushed

1 tbs extra virgin olive oil

1 cucumber, sliced finger size thick

1 cup pineapple, cut into chunks

1 tbs honey

1 heaping tsp corn flour

Method

1. Make cuts on the fish.

2. Steam fish in a steamer.

3. Heat oil in a pan; fry the garlic and onions till brown.

4. Add cucumber, pineapple, tomatoes, red chilli, soy sauce, and fish sauce. Add some pepper and mix in some honey to sweeten.

5. Mix in corn flour to thicken this mix.

6. Plate fish and add this mix on top of the fish.

7. Serve warm.

Flavourful soba with fish and vegetables

SERVES 2

Ingredients

2 fillets of any fish (preferably boneless)

100 grams of soba noodles (buckwheat), cooked in hot water

1–2 cups vegetable stock

½ to 1 tbs of soy sauce

1 inch piece ginger, cut into strips

2 green onions, side cut

1 red bell pepper, deseeded and skinned (post roasting), cut into strips

1 carrot, cut thin, finger size

3–4 pieces of bamboo shoots, cut into strips

4 bok choy leaves, cut into strips

1 tsp toasted sesame oil

Fistful of coriander leaves

Sea salt to taste or miso (1 tsp)

Method

1. Steam fish, after brushing with some oil.

2. Boil vegetable stock, add soy sauce, ginger, and all the vegetables and bring to a boil. Reduce heat and simmer for 5 minutes.

3. Add toasted sesame oil.
4. Add miso or sea salt at this point.
5. Divide noodles and spoon the vegetable broth over the noodles. Place the fish on top.
6. Garnish with coriander leaves

Asian salmon with brown rice

SERVES 2

Ingredients

½ to 1 inch piece of ginger
2 garlic cloves, minced
½ carrot, thinly sliced
2½ cups mushrooms, sliced
2 tbsp coriander, chopped
2 tsp honey
2 fish steaks (any)
1 tsp Chinese 5 spice powder
1 tbs soy sauce

Chinese 5 spice powder

1 tsp of pepper (Schezwan pepper preferred)
1 tsp of ground star anise
1 tsp ground fennel seeds
½ tsp ground cloves
½ tsp ground cinnamon
½ tsp sea salt
¼ tsp white pepper

Combine all the ingredients after dry roasting and grind together (optional) or let it stay whole.

Method

1. Marinate the fish (after washing), in the Chinese 5 spice powder, by smearing on either side of the fish steaks.

2. Steam or broil the fish steaks for 10 minutes, turn each side when halfway done.

3. Heat a pan; add soy sauce, ginger, garlic, ginger, honey, carrots and warm through for 4-5 minutes, until it softens. Add mushrooms and sauté for 2–3 minutes.

4. Season with sea salt and white pepper.

5. Plate warm brown rice, add vegetables on top and the fish. Garnish with chopped coriander.

Passionate pan fried fish with ras-el-hanout

SERVES 2

Ingredients

2 fish fillets

1 tsp ground cumin

1 tsp ras-el-hanout (Moroccan spice blend)

1 tsp cayenne pepper (can cut back, as ras-el-hanout has the cayenne)

1 tbs olive oil

Sea salt and ground pepper to taste

Ras-el-hanout

½ tsp of cayenne pepper

½ tsp of ground anise seeds (saunf)

¼ tsp ground cloves

2 tsp ground ginger (sonth)

2 tsp ground mace (javitri)

2 tsp ground cardamom

1 tsp cinnamon

1 tsp ground garam masala

1 tsp ground coriander seeds

1 tsp ground nutmeg

1 tsp turmeric

½ tsp each of white and black pepper

Dry roast all spices, blend together in a dry grinder

Method

1. Pre heat oven to 200 degrees Celsius.

2. Mix the spices together and marinate the fish in it by smearing on both sides. Let it sit for a half hour.

3. Heat oil in a pan and add the fish fillets. Cook till they change colour.

4. Steam any vegetable of your choice (options: cauliflower or sweet potatoes) and then cook with garlic—once cooked, blend together in a blender.

5. Divide into 2 plates and spoon fish on the side. Serve with green beans (steamed).

Aphrodisiacal seafood and eggplant salad

SERVES 2

Ingredients

150 gms of cooked prawns, mussels, and oysters

3 eggplants, sliced long, then cubed

2 fistfuls of coriander leaves, chopped

Dressing

1 tbs fish sauce

1 grated lime zest and juice

2–3 kafir lime leaves

1 tbs honey

1 tsp olive oil

1–2 dry red chillies

2 tbs of dried shrimp

Blend the dressing ingredients in a blender

Method

1. Brush the eggplant with some oil and cook in a pan till well done.

2. To this add the sea food.

3. Toss salad with dressing.

4. Garnish with coriander leaves.

Sizzling Thai-style fish

SERVES 2

Ingredients

2 boneless fish steaks, steamed and cubed

2 garlic cloves, crushed

1½ tsp turmeric

1½ tsp anise (saunf), powdered

2 red chillies, sliced long

1–2 inch piece of ginger, sliced

Grated zest of 1 lime and juice

1 tbs Thai fish sauce

1 tbs of soy sauce

1 cup coconut milk

Method

1. Marinate fish with turmeric, garlic, ginger, lime zest, and add soy sauce, fish sauce, and lime juice.

2. Heat a skillet and add some oil. Then add the fish pieces, cover, and cook for 2–3 minutes. Make sure the fish cooks on all sides.

3. Add the coconut milk once fish is done. Simmer for 15 minutes.

4. Garnish with sliced red chillies.

Aura-cleanse Asian stir fry

SERVES 4

Ingredients

3 cup green moong sprouts

2 cups cabbage, shredded

3 stalks of celery, chopped

½ cups cashews, halved

8 ounce block of tofu, cubed

1 green bell pepper, minced

3 tbs arrowroot powder

Sea salt to taste

Method

1. Heat olive oil in a wok, and brown tofu on either side.

2. Add the cashew nuts and brown them as well.

3. Remove from wok, add celery and the other vegetables, and stir fry. You can sprinkle some water.

4. Make sure vegetables don't wilt and remain crisp.

5. Add arrowroot powder by first diluting it in water.
6. Stir in the tofu.

Whole spaghetti and pure meat-less meat balls

SERVES 6

Ingredients

500 grams whole wheat pasta or spaghetti

3 cups cooked kidney beans

½ cup cooked brown rice

2 garlic cloves, minced

½ cup onion, diced

2 tbs tomato paste

1 tbs Worcestershire sauce

½ tsp oregano

½ tsp thyme

½ tsp basil

½ cup bread crumbs

1 tbs olive oil

8 servings of Marinara sauce (see recipe below)

Method

1. Cook pasta al dente.
2. Purée beans and rice in a food processor. It needs some texture, so don't purée into a fine paste.
3. Add onion, garlic, 1 tbs of olive oil, Worcestershire sauce, oregano, basil, and thyme.
4. Mix well either with your hands or a spoon. Add the bread crumbs.
5. Roll into small-size balls.

6. You can choose to shallow fry them, or bake at 175 degrees Celsius for ½ an hour.

7. Serve on top of spaghetti and marinara sauce.

Marinara sauce

SERVED 8

Ingredients

2 tbs extra virgin olive oil

4 garlic cloves, minced

1 red onion, diced

¼ tsp red pepper flakes

1 kilo tomatoes, roasted and chopped

½ cup tomato paste

1 tbs balsamic vinegar

2 tsp honey

2 tbs fresh basil, chopped

Sea salt and black pepper to taste

Method

1. Heat olive oil in a deep pan.

2. Sauté onion and garlic for about 7 minutes.

3. Add thyme, red pepper flakes, and oregano.

4. Add tomatoes and tomato paste.

5. Reduce heat and simmer for 30 minutes.

6. Add honey, balsamic vinegar, and sea salt. Simmer for 5–10 minutes.

7. Store in refrigerator for up to 5 days.

Divine burrito with black beans

SERVES 6

Ingredients

1 cup brown rice, cooked

2 tbsp extra virgin olive oil

1 yellow bell pepper, deseeded and cut into strips

1 red bell pepper, roasted, deseeded and cut into strips

1 onion, sliced into half moons

1 tbsp chilli powder

2 tsp cumin powder

½ tsp sea salt

½ kilo tomatoes, roasted and chopped

2 cups black beans, cooked

6 tortillas

Some avocado and salsa

Method

1. Heat olive oil in a pan. Sauté peppers and onions for about 7 minutes.

2. Add dry spices. Sauté for about 10 minutes.

3. Add tomatoes, lower heat, and cook for 7 minutes.

4. Pour into a bowl and add beans and rice, stir well.

5. To assemble: Heat tortillas until warm. Add 1 big serving spoon of peppers and onion mixture. Then layer with avocado and salsa. Roll and serve.

SERVES 4

Ingredients

1 tbs olive oil

2 cloves of garlic, minced

1 onion, diced

1 cup quinoa, cooked

2 cups mushrooms (mixed mushrooms if possible)

1 tbs red wine vinegar

2 tbs parsley, chopped

Juice of 1 lemon

1 tsp oregano

½ cup toasted walnuts or pine nuts

Sea salt and black pepper to taste

Method

1. Heat olive oil in a large pan and sauté garlic and onion.
2. Add mushrooms and vinegar and season with sea salt and pepper.
3. Cook for 5 minutes until mushrooms are soft.
4. Mix in parsley, oregano, and toasted nuts.
5. Toss in the quinoa and mix well.
6. Squeeze lime juice before serving.

Quintessential quesadillas

SERVES 4

Ingredients

1 red bell pepper, chopped fine

1 green bell pepper, chopped fine

1 head of corn, pressure cooked and blended in a mixer

4 ounces of tofu

1 chopped avocado

2 tbs olive oil

4 corn rotis (makai rotis)

Sea/rock salt to taste

Method

7. Put warm oil in a skillet.

8. Add green and red bell peppers. After a few minutes add the corn, and sauté for 5-7 minutes.

9. In the end, mix in avocado (can cream as well in a blender to achieve creamy consistency). Add salt and pepper.

10. Layer this mixture on one corn roti, while the roti is on the tava (flat cast iron pan). Grate tofu over this mix and sandwich with another roti.

11. Keep dry roasting it till it hardens a bit and remove from pan.

12. Then cut into 4 halves.

13. Enjoy with homemade tomato sauce.

Scrumptious whole wheat spaghetti with lemon and olives

SERVES 4

Ingredients

500 gms spaghetti (whole wheat)

4–5 garlic pods, thinly sliced

½ cup green or black olives

4 asparagus sticks, cut into 3 (boiled)

½ cup fresh basil, chopped

Sea salt and black pepper to taste

1 tbs olive oil

½ cup chopped tomatoes

Grated tofu (optional)

Method

1. Take some water and add spaghetti. Boil the water till al dente (cooked firm, but not too soft).

2. Cool after removing it and straining the water. Pour some cold water over it to prevent sticking.

3. Heat some oil and add garlic. Sauté for 5 minutes over low heat.

4. Add tomatoes, and after a few minutes, the asparagus. Sauté for 2–3 minutes.

5. Add spaghetti to this sauté and mix in the olives.

6. You have the option to grate some tofu on top.

Greens salad

SERVES 4

Ingredients

Any leafy greens, a bunch about 8–10 leaves

1 tbs red wine vinegar

1 tbs shallots (Madras onions)

½ tsp mustard

Sea salt and black pepper to taste

Walnuts (optional)

Method

1. Whisk together the red vinegar, shallots, mustard, sea salt, and black pepper.

2. Toss in with greens.

3. Can add walnuts at the end.

Merry moroccan veggies

SERVES 6

Ingredients

Grated lemon zest of 1 lemon

1½ tbs grated ginger

1 onion, sliced long

½ tsp cinnamon powder

2 ½ tsp coriander (dhaniya) powder

2 ½ tsp cumin (jeera) powder

½ tsp saffron threads (optional)

3 garlic cloves, crushed or grated

2 turnips (shalgam) cut in quarters

3 carrots cut in chunks

250 gms red pumpkin (bhopla) cut into chunks

½ eggplant cut into quarters (soak in water till not using to cook)

3 tomatoes, chopped

Sea salt and black pepper to taste

Some red chilli powder

Method

1. Take a heavy cast iron pot. Add the veggies, spices, and a little water. Cover and cook for 10 minutes. The veggies will cook in their own juices as well.

2. The eggplant can be sautéed separately in a wok with some olive oil.

3. Add the tomatoes to the cast iron veggies, cover, and cook for another 5 minutes.

4. Mix in the eggplant.

5. Serve with cooked quinoa.

6. You can make your quinoa interesting by adding green peas and making a dressing by tossing 1 tbs olive oil, ½ tsp cumin and turmeric powder, and some lime juice and blending in a mixer and tossing into the quinoa.

Rapturesque refried beans with corn tortillas and marinated bell peppers (as filling)

Refried beans

SERVES 6

Ingredients

2 cups red kidney beans

3 tbs olive oil

2 cups minced onion

6 garlic cloves, minced

2 tsp cumin

1½ tsp salt

Black pepper

1 small green bell pepper, minced

Method

1. Heat oil. Add onion, garlic, cumin, and salt. Add green bell pepper and sauté for 15 minutes.

2. Mash beans, as it always helps before adding to the sauté.

3. Turn heat to low and mix well.

Marinated bell peppers

SERVES 6

Ingredients

6 bell peppers (2 of each colour—red, green, and yellow)

½ tsp sea salt

½ tsp basil

½ tsp oregano

2 tbsp olive oil

2 garlic cloves, minced

2 tbsp red wine vinegar

Method

1. Roast only red bell peppers, make them sweat (see nifty fact sheet on how to make them sweat), and remove skin.

2. Cut all the peppers into thin strips.

3. Heat oil in deep dish skillet and add herbs, sea salt, garlic and black peppers, and peppers.

4. Coat peppers with oil and sauté for 5 minutes only.

5. Remove from gas, and mix in red wine vinegar.

6. Store overnight or for at least 1 hour while kept covered.

7. Better to serve chilled as it makes for a great filling as well as with the tortillas with the beans.

Craving chickpea salad

SERVES 4

Ingredients

1 onion, diced

1 each of red, yellow, and green bell pepper, diced

(remove skin of red pepper)

2 cups cooked chickpeas

2 bundles bok choy, cut long and steamed

Olives (optional)

Dressing

¼ cup olive oil

3 tbs balsamic vinegar

3 garlic cloves, minced

Grated zest of 1 lime and juice

Sea salt to taste

Method

1. Get the ingredients together in a salad bowl.
2. Heat oil and add garlic, then remove from heat and whisk in balsamic vinegar and lime juice with zest and sea salt.
3. Toss into salad.
4. Chill before serving.

Stamina stuffed quinoa bell peppers

SERVES 8

Ingredients

4 yellow and red bell peppers

¾ cup quinoa

¼ cup black currants

2 cups water

1 cup black beans (rajma)

2 cups chopped spinach

2 cloves garlic, minced

2 cups tomatoes, diced

1 tsp coriander

2 tsp cumin

2 celery stalks

1 onion, diced

2 tbsp olive oil

Sea salt to taste

Method

1. Heat pan and add olive oil, onion, celery, and garlic.

2. Then add the dry spices, and cook for 5 minutes until the onions get soft.

3. Add tomatoes and sea salt. Cook for another 5 minutes.

4. Stir in black beans, black currants, and quinoa with 2 cups of water and bring to a boil.

5. Reduce heat to low and let it simmer for about 20 minutes, until quinoa absorbs water.

6. Pre-heat oven to 175 degrees Celsius.

7. Fill each bell pepper with ¼ cup quinoa.

8. Place in a baking dish and cover with foil.

9. Bake for 10 minutes until you see the tops have turned brown.

10. Remove from oven and let the bell peppers sit for 10 minutes before serving.

Favoured fusilli salad

SERVES 4

Ingredients

300 gms dried whole wheat fusilli

150 gms green beans, cut in 1 inch lengths

1 small avocado, diced

1 red bell pepper, roasted, skinned, and diced

400 gms white soya beans, cooked and drained

4–5 mounaka raisins, de-seeded

Ingredients and method for dressing

2 tsp curry powder

1 tsp cumin

8 tbs soy yogurt

8 tbs tofu mayonnaise

3 tbs lime juice

Sea salt and black pepper

Whisk all ingredients in a blender together to form a thick, creamy dressing.

Method

1. Cook fusilli in boiling water till al dente.
2. Blanch green beans in boiling water for 5 minutes.
3. Put together cooked fusilli, green beans, soya beans, and avocado.
4. Add dressing and chill before serving.

Tantalizing tofu and broccoli in sweet and sour sauce

SERVES 4

Ingredients

100 gms mushrooms, preferably shitake

(Soak mushrooms in water and slice long)

300 gms tofu, cubed after steaming

1 medium onion, diced

1 inch ginger, chopped fine

1 garlic clove, minced

1 tsp sesame oil

1 carrot, sliced thin like matchsticks

200 gms broccoli florets

Sea salt and black pepper

For the sauce

1½ cups vegetable stock

2 tbs agave syrup (or stevia)

3 cups chopped tomato

2 tbs soy sauce

2 tbs vinegar (preferably apple cider)

1½ tbs arrowroot powder

Some water

Method

1. Blanch broccoli and carrots in hot water.

2. Heat oil, add garlic, ginger, tofu, and sauté for 5 minutes.

3. Add vegetables and sprinkle with salt and pepper. Add vegetable stock, vinegar, soya sauce, and tomatoes. Bring to a boil. Let it simmer for 3 minutes.

4. Dissolve arrowroot powder in water and stir into the vegetables.

5. Serve warm.

Surreal shrimp chilli basil

SERVES 2

Ingredients

2 garlic pods, minced

2 tbs cold pressed coconut oil

1 green chilli, chopped

6 shrimps (prawns) medium size, deveined and shelled

1 tbs Thai fish sauce

1 onion, sliced thin

1 tbs soy sauce (no sodium preferable)

15–20 fresh basil leaves

Sweet to taste, use stevia or honey

Method

1. Heat oil in a wok. Add garlic, onions (sauté for 2-3 minutes). Add chillies and stir fry till onions are translucent.

2. Stir fry for 2 minutes, till shrimp is tender.

3. Serve with brown rice and a salad.

Quinoa pilaf

SERVES 2

Ingredients

½ cup quinoa, rinse well

1 cup water or vegetable stock

1–2 garlic pods, minced

1 medium onion, sliced thinly

1 red bell pepper, de-seeded, roasted, with skin removed and diced

½ tsp each of turmeric, cumin (jeera powder), coriander (dhaniya)

½ cup cooked chickpeas (optional)

Cardamom (elaichi) powder

1 fistful of coriander leaves

1 fistful of mint leaves

Sea salt and pepper to taste

1 tbs olive oil

Method

1. Add quinoa to boiling water or vegetable stock; cover and simmer till cooked.

2. Add oil to a frying pan or skillet. Add onions, garlic, red bell pepper, and chickpeas. Cook for about 3–4 minutes.

3. Add quinoa to this veggie mix. Season with sea salt and pepper.

4. Stir in coriander and mint before serving.

Tenacious tuna and tomato salad

SERVES 2

Ingredients

1 can of tuna, shredded

2 green onions, thinly sliced

Some chives, fresh or dried

1 tomato, diced

Juice of ½ lime

Sea salt and pepper to taste

Dressing

2–3 tbs of tofu mayonnaise

Method

1. Shred tofu in a bowl with your hands.

2. Add green onions, chives, and tomato.

3. Season with dried or fresh chives, sea salt, and pepper, and mix in tofu mayonnaise.

Creamy vegan tofu

SERVES 6

Ingredients

1 pack of mori nu silken tofu or tofu which has a creamy
   consistency—you may need to add soy milk to get this

2 tbs lemon juice

1 tsp miso (white)

2 tsp olive oil

Method

1. Steam tofu in a steamer for 3–5 minutes; let it cool a bit.

2. Add all the ingredients to and whip together and voila!

3. Variations: sometimes I add 1 tsp of mustard to give it a twist (especially good for your liver when you do this).

Gratifying Goan prawn curry

SERVES 4

Ingredients

3–4 garlic cloves, minced

1 tsp chilli powder

1 tbs coriander powder

½ tsp turmeric

1 tsp ginger, grated

1–2 tbs tamarind, soaked in water and paste removed

500 gms prawns, deveined and shelled

Handful of spinach

3 tbs coconut milk

Sea salt and black pepper to taste

Method

1. In a skillet, mix spices with tamarind to a paste. Add garlic, 1½ cups water, and bring to a boil. Let it simmer for up to 10 minutes, until sauce becomes thick.
2. When flame is on low, add coconut milk and then add prawns. Cook for 2–3 minutes. Just stir in spinach in the end, and cook for 3–4 minutes.
3. Serve with brown rice.

Fish burgers

SERVES 4

Ingredients

2 fillets of any fish, steamed
½ cup regular flour
½ cup bread crumbs
Sea salt, black pepper, and a dash of mustard

Method

1. In a bowl combine fish, flour, and bread crumbs with sea salt, pepper, and mustard.
2. Shape into burger croquettes.
3. Pan fry in a non-stick frying pan.

For fillers:

Use sliced cucumber, tomato, and lettuce. Assemble the burgers by first toasting the buns, then spreading tofu mayonnaise on the buns, and then layering the fish burgers with the veggies.

Succulent steamed basa

SERVES 2

Ingredients

    2 pieces of basa
    Juice of 1 lime
    1 tbs olive oil
    1 tbs garlic-ginger paste
    Sea salt and black pepper to taste

Method

1. Take a knife and make thin cuts on the basa fillets.
2. Mix all the above ingredients and smear on both sides of the fish.
3. Keep in the fridge for about 2 hours.
4. Steam before you want to eat the fish for about 7 minutes.

Bashful baked mushrooms with tomato and garlic

SERVES 2

Ingredients

    225 gms mushrooms
    1–2 celery sticks, chopped
    2 tomatoes, chopped
    3 garlic cloves, minced
    ½ cup bread crumbs
    1 tbs dried herbs (any)
    2 tbs shredded tofu
    ½ cup vegetable stock
    Sea salt and black pepper to taste

Method

1. Heat a pan, then add mushrooms, cover and let them cook till done (they leave water and will cook in this water).

2. Heat a wok and add some oil. Add the cooked mushrooms, celery, garlic, and sauté them. After 3–4 minutes, turn off the gas and allow to cool.

3. Mix bread crumbs, tomatoes, and dried herbs of your choice.

4. Layer the mushrooms in a casserole dish, pour some vegetable stock in the dish, then add the bread crumb mixture on top of the mushrooms.

5. Bake in an oven for about 10 minutes at 180 degrees Celsius.

6. Pull the dish out after 10 minutes and add shredded tofu on top and bake again for 5 minutes.

SOUPS

Cauliflower and red pepper soup

SERVES 4

Ingredients

3 cups cauliflower, cut into medium size pieces

½ tsp extra virgin olive oil

1 small red bell pepper, roasted de-skinned and diced small

½ an onion, diced

1½ cups boiling water

½ green onion, sliced sideways for garnish

Method

1. Heat oil in a pan (deep pan), sauté onion first, for about 15 minutes.

2. Remove onion and then sauté cauliflower for 4-5 minutes.

3. Add the water and cover.Simmer until cauliflower is tender, about 10 minutes.

4. Cool, and transfer this mixture to a blender. Process until smooth; add more water if required.

5. Return to the soup pot and simmer for 3 minutes.

6. Serve with red bell pepper and green onions as garnish.

Spicy sensual tomato soup

SEVES 6

Ingredients

3 medium fresh tomatoes, diced

1 tbs tofu mayonnaise

1 tbsp honey (optional)

2 cups water

Lots of fresh ground black pepper

1½ cups onions, minced

4 garlic cloves, crushed

½ tsp sea salt

1 tsp dill

2 cups water or vegetable stock

1 tbs olive oil

Parsley or basil (fresh) for garnish

Method

1. Heat oil and add onions, garlic, salt, dill, and black pepper. Sauté for about 5-8 minutes, till onions get soft.

2. Add tomatoes, water, and honey. Cover and let it simmer for 20 minutes.

3. Whisk in tofu mayonnaise 5 minutes before serving. Sprinkle some parsley or basil for garnish.

Pumpkin soup

SERVES 2

Ingredients

250 gms red pumpkin (bhopla/lal kaddu)
1 onion, diced
½ carrot, cubed
Pinch of cinnamon
Sea salt to taste

Method

1. Boil pumpkin, carrots, and onions together in 1 cup of water.
2. Add cinnamon and sea salt.
3. Once done, just blend with a hand blender.
4. Garnish with parsley before serving.

Lentil soup

SERVES 2

½ cup yellow lentils (pigeon pea [toovar] or channa [gram])
½ tsp cumin seeds
½ tsp turmeric
½ tsp red chilli flakes
1 cup vegetable stock
1 tsp cardamom seeds
1 tsp mustard seeds
½ onion, sliced into half moons
1 garlic pod, crushed
Sea salt to taste
Or 1 tsp white miso instead

Method

1. Pressure cook lentils with cumin, chilli flakes, and purée once done.
2. Heat oil in a pan. Add mustard and cardamom seeds, fry till they pop. Then add the onion and garlic and cook till it browns a bit.
3. Mix in with the lentils and give it a stir.
4. Once lentil soup is ready, you can add the miso paste or sea salt to taste.

Carrot and dal soup

SERVES 2

Ingredients

½ onion, diced small
2 garlic clove, minced
2 tbs tomato puree
200 gms carrots, grated
¼ cup pink lentils (can take arhar dal), washed and set aside
½ cup vegetable stock
Fistful of coriander for garnishing
Sea salt or miso

Method

1. Heat oil and add onion and garlic. Cook till pink (about 4–5 minutes). Add tomato purée and cook for 1 minute.
2. Add carrots, lentils, and vegetable stock and boil.
3. Cook till the lentils and vegetables are done.
4. Blend once done.

5. Season with sea salt or add miso.

6. Garnish with coriander.

Flamboyant fish and noodle soup

SERVES 2

Ingredients

½ packet of soba, udon, or rice noodles

2 pieces of boneless fish

1 tbs of fish sauce

1 tbs sesame (toasted preferable) oil

Sea salt and black pepper to taste

2 cups vegetable stock

Toppings: green onion (side cut), coriander leaves, lime
wedges, ground peanut, red spicy chutney

Method

1. Boil vegetable stock.

2. Prepare noodles separately.

3. Heat some oil in a skillet. Add fish, fish sauce, and stir fry for
2–3 minutes.

4. Divide noodles among two bowls. First put the fish on top,
then pour the stock.

5. Top up the dish with your selection of toppings.

SNACKS AND DESSERTS

Sensual super food trail mix

SERVES 4

Ingredients

- 3 tbs pumpkin seeds
- 3 tbs sunflower seeds
- 2/3 rd cup dried apricots
- ½ cup walnuts, dry roasted and chopped
- 6 tbs dried berries (any: sugar free)
- 4 tbs dried coconut

Method

1. Roast seeds.
2. Mix in a bowl with apricots, walnuts, berries, and coconut.
3. Store in an airtight container in the fridge .
4. Can be stored for 15 days.

Attraction-building almond, fig, and cacao bars

SERVES 6

Ingredients

- ¼ cup any nuts
- ¼ cup almonds
- ¼ cup rolled oats
- ½ cup dried apricots
- ½ cup dried figs
- 1 tbs cacao (cocoa) powder

2½ tbs orange juice (fresh)

1 tbs dried coconut

Method

1. Soak figs and apricots in the orange juice.

2. Heat oven to 180 degrees Celsius.

3. On a baking sheet put all nuts for up to 8 minutes in the oven.

4. Bake oats for 5 minutes.

5. Cool both nuts and oats.

6. Process both nuts and oats in a grinder.

7. Process the figs, apricots, orange juice and cacao powder into a purée.

8. Mix oats, coconut, and the puréed fruit together.

9. Line a baking pan with butter/baking paper, and spread this mix on the pan evenly about ½ inch in thickness.

10. Chill in the refrigerator for up to an hour, and once set, cut into bars and store in the fridge for up to one week.

Gluten free chocolate cake

SERVES 10

Ingredients

2 tbs extra virgin olive oil

200 gms dark baking chocolate

1 cup soy milk

2 tbs cocoa powder

4 tbs agave syrup or stevia

1 tsp vanilla essence

¼ cup brown rice flour or sorghum (jovar) flour

4 tbs Vegan egg substitute (optional)

1 cup ground almonds

1 tbs baking powder (preferable aluminium-free)

Method

1. Preheat oven to 180 degrees Celsius.

2. Melt chocolate in a double boiler and cool.

3. Heat milk with agave syrup. Add flour and cocoa powder. Pour into a bowl and stir in the chocolate and oil.

4. Add the egg substitute to the mix.

5. Mix well either with a spatula or an electric mixer at high speed.

6. Pour into a cake tin (after greasing tin with oil) and bake for 40 minutes.

7. Serves well as brownies (when cut into squares), with the dairy-free ice cream (see recipe).

Heavenly poached pears

SERVES 2

Ingredients

2 pears peeled

¼ cup raisins

2 tbsp roasted walnuts, chopped

1 cinnamon stick

1 tsp agave syrup

Juice of 1 lime

¼ cup apple juice

Method

1. Cut pears into half and scoop middle out with a spoon.

2. Soak raisins in lime and apple juice; add cinnamon to the juice.

3. Fill centre of pears with soaked raisins (retain juice) and walnuts.

4. Cover with a foil, pack tightly.

5. Steam for 10 minutes or you can even bake for 15 minutes at 200 degrees Celsius.

6. Open and pour juice that is left of raisins over the pears before serving.

Lustful raw chocolate bars

SERVES 2

Ingredients

3 tbs cocoa powder

4 tbs cooking dark chocolate

2 tbs agave syrup

1 tsp vanilla essence

¼ cup pecans or walnuts, roasted and chopped

¼ cup pistachios, cut into half

½ cup dried apricots (optional)

Grated zest of 1 orange

Method

1. Melt dark cooking chocolate in a double boiler.

2. Once it has melted, stir in agave syrup and vanilla essence.

3. Stir in the nuts and orange zest.

4. Line a baking dish with butter paper, pour the chocolate mix, and chill for a couple of hours.

5. Break into pieces, and store in a container in the fridge for up to 2–15 days.

Wild berry compote

SERVES 2

Ingredients

1½ cup frozen mixed berries

Pinch of cinnamon

1 tsp agave syrup

1 tsp arrowroot powder

1½ cup soy yogurt

Method

1. Take berries, agave syrup, cinnamon and 1 tbs water and warm in a pan. Cover and simmer for approximately 5 minutes.
2. Mix arrowroot powder with cold water, and add to the pan berry mixture.
3. Let the mixture cool.
4. Serve with chilled soy yogurt. You can add a few raisins or some honey, if desired.

Romantic strawberry and banana non-dairy ice cream

SERVE 2

Ingredients

2 bananas, chopped and frozen

10 strawberries, frozen

1 cup almond milk, frozen in an ice tray

Method

1. Remove the frozen fruit and almond milk.
2. Blend together in a blender.
3. Add some honey or agave syrup if desired.
4. You can also add some pistachios.

Heavenly coconut ice cream

SERVES 8

Ingredients

2 cups coconut milk (full fat)

1 cup cashews soaked for ½ hour

1 tbs vanilla essence

¼ cup agave syrup or honey

¼ cup shredded coconut

¼ tsp of sea salt

¼ cup coconut oil

Method

1. Blend all the ingredients together in a blender on high speed until creamy.
2. Pour into an ice-cream maker and make into an ice cream or freeze into an ice tray as is.

Ambrosia pear and fig compote

SERVES 2

Ingredients

2 pears, cored and cut into wedges

½ cup dried apricots

½ cup dried figs

10 cardamom pods, crushed

5 tbs soy yogurt

1 tsp pumpkin seeds (unsalted)

Method

1. Put all the ingredients in a pan. Cover and cook for 5 minutes.

2. Cover and chill in the refrigerator overnight.

3. Discard cardamom pods and divide the mix between 2 bowls, then add the soy yogurt from the top and pumpkin seeds.

Fig apple compote

SERVES 4

Ingredients

1 cup fresh figs, chopped

1 apple, cut into chunks

1 pear, cut into chunks

2 tbs raisins

Pinch of cinnamon

Method

1. Put warm fruit and spices in a pan. You can add ¼ cup water or apple juice.

2. Stir frequently.

3. Serve warm.

Happy baked curried bananas

SERVES 2

Ingredients

2 bananas (can use Kerala bananas)
2 tbs lime juice
2 tbs honey
1 tbs ghee

Method

1. Peel bananas, cut into bit-size pieces.
2. Steam bananas.
3. Pour hot ghee over the bananas, and then lime juice and honey.
4. Bake at 200 degrees Celsius for 5–10 minutes (optional).

Greens dip

Yields 2 cups

Ingredients

3 green onions, chopped
1½ cups cashews, soaked for 2 hours
3 tbs parsley
3 tbs coriander
1 tbs honey mustard
1 tbs apple cider vinegar (optional)
2 tsp white miso (optional)
2 tsp honey
Sea salt to taste
Juice of ½ a lime
3 tbs extra virgin olive oil
Water

Method

1. Purée all the ingredients in a food processor.
2. Add water to thin down the paste, and add olive oil from the top, while the food processor is still running. This makes the paste creamier.
3. Make sure all ingredients are well blended.

Robust roasted spiced mixed nuts

YIELDS 2 CUPS

Ingredients

2 tbs rosemary, chopped

2 tbs agave syrup or honey

½ tsp red chilli powder

2 tbs extra virgin olive oil

¼ tsp cinnamon

1 tbs sea salt (coarse)

½ cup walnuts

½ cup pecans

½ cup pistachios

½ cup almonds

Method

1. Preheat oven to 175 degrees Celsius.
2. In a pan combine all the ingredients, but not the nuts.
3. Add the nuts and toss well, until all the ingredients are combined.
4. Spread over a baking sheet or butter paper.
5. Bake for 12–15 minutes, stirring halfway through.
6. Allow to cool.

Passionate fruit jello

SERVES 2

Ingredients

1½ cup fruit juice (freshly squeezed)
2 tbs honey
½ cup lemon juice
1 tbs agar flakes (plain china grass)
1 cup fruit, bite-sized pieces

Method

1. Cut the fruit and set aside.
2. Stir the agar flakes into half of the fruit juice and let it sit for 2 minutes.
3. Add the honey and stir well.
4. Use a deep pan and bring this mix to a boil.
5. Keep stirring, remove from gas, and add the rest of the juice.
6. Cool at room temperature.
7. Stir in the fruit; refrigerate until it sets.

Joyful fruit salad

SERVES 6

Ingredients

1 large pear, cubed
1 cup fresh grapes, remove seeds, cut in half
1 apple, cubed
1 cup berries (any)
½ cup cashew pieces

½ tsp vanilla essence

Pinch of saffron

2 tbs honey

Tofu cream (optional)

Method

1. Mix all the above ingredients and serve.

2. Optional to serve with the tofu cream. You can make tofu cream by whipping silken tofu [steamed] with some honey in a blender.

Orange agar gel

SERVES 4

Ingredients

3¼ cup orange juice (freshly squeezed)

2 tbs honey

2 tbs agar flakes

2 cups chopped fruit

Method

1. Cut the fruit.

2. Stir agar flakes into half the juice and let it sit for 2 minutes.

3. Add the honey and bring to a boil and stir for 2 minutes.

4. Remove from the heat and add the rest of the juice.

5. Cool at room temperature and stir in the fruit.

6. Refrigerate until set.

Sweet nectar ambrosia

SERVES 8

Ingredients

1 cup oranges, bite-sized pieces

1 cup pineapple, cubed

1 cup grapes, de-seeded and cut into half

1 cup coconut

½ cup cashews

1 tbs orange or lemon rind

2 tbs agar flakes

1 cup cold water

⅓ cup honey

1 cup fruit juice

1 cup soy yogurt

Method

1. Cut the fruit.
2. Stir in the agar flakes into water and let it sit for 2 minutes.
3. Add the honey.
4. Bring to a boil and boil for 2 minutes, stirring continuously.
5. Remove from the heat and cool at room temperature.
6. Stir in all the remaining ingredients.
7. Refrigerate until set.

Grape and pineapple jello

SERVES 4

Ingredients

2¾ cups grape juice

1½ tbs agar flakes

1½ cups pineapple, cubed

Method

1. Cut the fruit into pieces.
2. Stir in the agar flakes into half the juice.
3. Add the honey.
4. Boil the mix for 2 minutes, stirring continuously.
5. Remove from the heat and cool at room temperature.
6. Stir in the chopped fruit.
7. Refrigerate and chill until set.

Source List

Dr Bharathi Chawathe
+91 22 26499461
+91 22 26001044
E mail: admin@springnature.org
www.springnature.org

Dr Divya Chhabra
+91 22 26204412

Zia Lambrou
Craniosacral Therapist
+91 9821470396
www.quantacare.org

Dr Shiv Bajaj and Dr Anuja Singh
Bak2Health Clinic
+91 8130804444

Nifty Fact Sheet

1. The words *al dente* come from the Italian term 'to the tooth' or 'to the bite', referring to when the Italians needed to chew the pasta due to its firmness

2. Warming olive oil and adding onions to it before the oil actually warms up, will retain the smell and flavour of the olive oil in your food

3. Sticking your greens in ice cold water before adding it to your salad will make them nice and perky

4. You can make red bell peppers sweat by roasting them on an open flame, like your home burner. Then put them in any biodegradable bag and knot the bag shut. This makes them sweat. Then under running water, remove skin, it comes off in a jiffy

5. If you cover a dish while baking, you need to make a fold in the foil paper in the centre—like a tent—to let the air circulate and the dish breathe

6. Ras-el-hanout is a Moroccan spice and translates literally as 'head of the shop'—a great spice for your love life

Bibliography

Claus Wedekind, 'The Sweaty T-Shirt Study' conducted in 1995.

Diane K. Osbone, 'Reflections on The Art of Living: A Joseph Campbell Companion' (Joseph Campbell Foundation, 1991)

Edward Esko, *Yin Yang Primer* (One Peaceful World Press, 2000)

Geneen Roth, *When Food is Love* (Plume, Published by the Penguin Group, 1989)

Havlicek J. and Lecnochova P., 'The effect of Meat Consumption on Body Odour Attractiveness,' Chemical Senses, 2006 October 31st 31(8), 747-52

Helen Fisher, *Anatomy of Love: A Natural History of Mating, Marriage and Why We Stray* (Ballantine Books, January 1994)

Katherine Eposito, MD, PhD and Dario Giugliano Md, PhD, 'Lifestyle and Dietary Recommendations for Erectile Dysfunction and Female Sexual Dysfunction,' by Urologic Clinic (Urologic.theclinics.com), 2011

James L Wislon, *Adrenal Fatigue: The 21st Century Stress Syndrome* (Smart Publications: CA, 2001)

Joy McClure and Kendall Layne, *Cooking for Consciousness* (Nucleus Publications, 1976)

Judith Anodea, *Wheels of Life* (Llewellyn Publications, USA, 1997)

Judith Anodea, *Eastern Body, Western Mind: Psychology of the Chakra System as a Path to the Self* (Celestial Arts Berkley, 1996)

Larry Young, *The Chemistry Between Us: Love, Sex and the Science of Attraction* (Penguin USA, 2012)

Lauman EO, Paik A, Rosen RC, 'Sexual Dysfunction in the United States: Prevalence and Predictors,' Journal of American Medical Association, 1999, Feb 10; 281(6):537-44

Louise Hay, *You Can Heal Your Life* (Faber, 2008)

Lutfey KE, Link CL, Rosen RC et al, 'Prevalence and correlates of sexual activity and function in women,' Boston Area Community Health survey (BACH), 2002-2005

Marnia Robinson, *Peace Between The Sheets: Healing with Sexual Relationships* (Frog Books, 2003)

Michio Kushi, *The Book of Macrobiotics* (Japan Publications, Inc., 1987)

Michio Kushi, *Your Body Never Lies* (Square One Publishers, 2007)

Mikhail Naimy, *The Book Of Mirdad* (Watkins Publishing London, 1983)

Robert Fried, Lynn Edlen-Nezin, *Great Food, Great Sex: The Three Food Factors for Sexual Fitness* (Ballantine Books, New York, 2006)

Rosemary Basson, Jennifer Berman, Arthur Burnett,et al., 'Report of the International Consensus Developmental Conference on Female Sexual Dysfunction,' The Journal of Urology, 2000, Vol. 163, Issue 3, 888-893

Shawn Talbott, *The Cortisol Connection: Why Stress Makes you Fat and Ruins Your Health-And What You Can do About It* (Publishers Group West, 2002)

Steve Gagne, *The Energetics of Food* (Healing Arts Press; 3 edition; 5 November 2008)

Zorgniotti, A. W, et al., 'Effect of the large doses of the Nitric oxide Precursor L-Arginine, on Erectile Dysfunction,' International Journal of Impotence Research, Vol 6 (1) March 1994 (33-35)

Acknowledgements

I WOULD LIKE TO BEGIN BY thanking my teacher and guide Mona Schwartz who bought me to my true calling in life. She's infused my life with everlasting love. I pray for her soul, and hope that I can continue to carry the bright torch of Macrobiotics in India.

S.N. Goenkaji, who nurtured the seed of Vipassana and helped me discover higher levels of myself. I pray for his soul and I'm indebted to him forever for giving me this wonderful technique to achieve enlightenment.

Gulzar uncle, for being a pillar of love in my father's life, and in mine.

My editor, Milee—her calm disposition and encouragement throughout the process of getting this book together was invaluable.

Hema Maliniji, Esha, and Ahana Deol—for giving me so much of love.

My clients and staff, for bringing in the love for what I believe in, that sustains me through each day.

Vilas and Nikki Naik, my cousins—for allowing me the luxury of moving to Goa for a month to finish my book in their wonderful villa, which is full of love.

My mom, for giving me that 'unconditionality' of love I thrive on, and my family—Vishal, Pooja, Shabana, Azaan,

Zaara, and Shiv—for bringing in humour and much needed daily doses of oxytocin!

Brian D'Souza, for supporting me at every level with my Macrobiotic endeavour and in my life.

Dr Bharathi Chawathe, for her love of my being and making me explore higher levels of love for myself.

Dr Divya Chabria, for resolving all my issues and making me understand how psychosomatic stuff can really impact health.

And finally, deep gratitude to the infinite 'universal life force' that supports me and keeps me in a state of love all the time.

A Note on the Author

SHONALI IS INDIA'S FIRST GRADUATE and practising Counsellor/
Chef and Instructor in Macrobiotics from the Kushi Institue,
USA and that is her USP. She is a celebrity counsellor and chef to
some of the hottest and fittest Bollywood beauties. Her clients
include and have includeed Hema Malini, Neha Dhupia, Esha
Deol, Ahana Deol, Jacqueline Fernandez, Zoya Akhtar, Katrina
Kaif, Tabu, Shekhar Kapur, Kabir Bedi, and Dalip Tahil.

Her tryst with macrobiotics began in 1998 when her father
was diagnosed with cancer, and she wanted to help him with an
alternative approach to recovery. She sought a diet that would
enhance one's 'well being' from within, focussing on changing
blood condition and using food as a tool to change any kind
of imbalances in the body and mind. She has been featured in
The Times of India, *Vogue*, *Elle*, *Hindustan Times*, MINT, *DNA,*
and so on.

She meets her clients' needs not only on the health
counselling level, but goes beyond that, wherein she equips you
with recipes, cooking classes, and helps you to source products.
She has her own line of retail products of ready-to-eat snacks
and treats under her brand name 'Soulfood'. She is soon to
launch a health café in Mumbai, which she plans to take all

over India. All of these products are vegetarian, organic, and free from dairy, gluten, yeast, sugar, white processed flour, and non GMOs.

She is the author of *The Beauty Diet*.

You can find out more at www.soulfoodshonalli.com